Business Processes for Business Communities

Frank Schönthaler • Gottfried Vossen
Andreas Oberweis • Thomas Karle

Business Processes
for Business Communities

Modeling Languages, Methods, Tools

Springer

Dr. Frank Schönthaler
PROMATIS software GmbH
Ettlingen
Germany

Prof. Dr. Gottfried Vossen
University of Münster
Information Systems
Münster
Germany

Prof. Dr. Andreas Oberweis
Karlsruhe Institute of Technology (KIT)
Institut AIFB
Hertzstr.
Karlsruhe
Germany

Thomas Karle
PROMATIS software GmbH
Business Applications Division
Ettlingen
Germany

The original German edition was published in 2010 by Oldenbourg Wissenschaftsverlag.

ISBN 978-3-642-43052-7   ISBN 978-3-642-24791-0 (eBook)
DOI 10.1007/978-3-642-24791-0
Springer Heidelberg Dordrecht London New York

Springer is part of Springer Science+Business Media (www.springer.com)

Preface

For my children, Sabrina and Marcel, who have always given me
the strength to master difficult challenges with confidence.

Frank Schönthaler

Inspired by first successful practical projects in Central European financial service and industrial enterprises, two of the authors of this book—Andreas Oberweis and Frank Schönthaler—started in the mid-1980s to develop methods and software tools for business process modeling. It may have been attributed to the aura of the time-honored Fridericiana University of Karlsruhe that a certain "sense of mission" quickly spread out among the team of ambitious young researchers; it was obvious that the whole world would soon use suitable methods and software tools to create business process models. And even more: These models would be created in a mathematically sound notation to be also amenable to formal analyses and optimizations. Not only the sequence of operations aspects should be described, but business processes should be included as a whole to be able to depict resource requirements, responsibilities, business objects, and much more. In short: The objective was to arrive at complete "business building plans" through business process models. And why should the design and optimization of enterprises not be as successful with what has been common practice for thousands of years in technical design? And usually the technical design has much less complex structures than what a business represents today. However, what was obvious to young researchers then had in reality not or only partially confirmed itself. Business processes are today's lynchpin, concerning changes in enterprises. Business reengineering, implementation of business software systems (ERP, CRM, SCM, etc.), business process management, governance, risk, and compliance management, just to mention a few current topics, are unthinkable without a thorough examination of business processes. In addition, all technical innovations are scrutinized first for their suitability to influence a customer's business processes in a positive manner. Indeed, varieties of business process tools have appeared on the market within the last decades. The authors of this book have themselves had the experts sit up and take notice with a promising high-end tool. Yet a glance cast behind the scenes and an analysis of the productive use of the tools causes quick disillusionment: While trained business process experts are using the tools successfully in enterprises and consulting firms, the majority of "business process workers" use the business process tool No. 1: Microsoft Office Suite! With adventurous description lists, cross-reference matrices, and informal schematic images, an attempt is launched to master the complexity of a company's business processes, to highlight potential for optimization, and to provide a solid basis for the development of supporting information systems. It may sound exaggerated, but the authors have seen, in practice, a number of such business process descriptions, which have been the basis of large-scale projects in the two-digit million Euro range. Quite a number of these projects, with which the clients had connected high hopes, expecting these to be the driver for further corporate development, ended up as a costly mistake.

These essential experiences in practice have been the starting point and the basis of an intensive exchange of ideas between the practice representatives, the college lecturers, and researchers in the authors' circle. Why is it that the use of business process tools remains limited to a relatively small circle of experts? Why do so many projects fail due to problems which obviously could have been avoided by using suitable methods and tools? What contribution can social networks make in connection with modern web technologies to promote the "business process culture" in the enterprises? But it should not remain with just the exchange of ideas to answer these pressing questions: In the research and developer network Horus® Endeavor™, groups from Karlsruhe Institute of Technology (Andreas Oberweis), the University of Münster (Gottfried Vossen), the University of Applied Sciences in Konstanz (Marco Mevius), the FZI Research Center for Computer Science in Karlsruhe, as well as the industrial partner Horus software GmbH, have joined forces to develop ideas for innovative business process methods and software tools. Results of this continuing research activity of several years have led to the development of the Horus® Method™ and Horus® business process tools. To preclude "cost barriers," the Horus® tools are freely accessible in a fully functional freeware version for research and education, and also for practical project use. In addition, a professional distribution (Horus Enterprise) can be obtained from Horus software GmbH.

But how can many potential users of business process instruments be possibly reached? To answer this question reliably, this target group must be clearly defined. The bottom line is: The target group proves to be extremely heterogeneous, if not "diffuse." Of course, it includes business consultants, organization and IT department employees, and, not to forget, management assistants. However, returning to our initial considerations, it becomes clear that specialists and executives in the business departments, who develop business process ideas and play a part in their implementation, also belong to the target group. They are often referred to as key users, as ultimately they are the key for the implementation of new business processes or process changes throughout the organization. The obvious diffusion of the target group has led us to the consideration that it is much easier to reach the potential users as part of their university education before being discharged into practice to pursue different career paths. Moreover, what could be better than providing a reference book that can be used as a basis for lectures and internships? This reference book should provide extensive practical experience, so that valuable support in practical work can be afforded. We would like to emphasize that the book is not primarily aimed at computer specialists and, therefore, requires no computer science knowledge. It is rather a business book that addresses management experts and industrial engineers as well as computer scientists, business information specialists and information experts, and also engineers in business process questions.

After a brief introduction to the topic, the book offers a quick start into model-based business process engineering in Chap. 2. In Chap. 3, the foundations of the modeling languages used are conveyed. Meaningful examples are in the foreground—each of the underlying formalisms is treated only as far as needed. Chapter 4 describes the Horus method. The book defines a sequence of activities which finally leads to the creation of a complete business process model. The Horus method, incidentally, is not bound to the use of the Horus software tools. It can be used with other tools or, if necessary, be used even without tool support. Important application fields of business process engineering are described in Chap. 5. The spectrum ranges from business process reengineering to the development and implementation of information systems. The book concludes with an outlook on the future of business process engineering and highlights current research activities of the Horus Endeavor partners.

The book can be read either in context or as a whole, and specifically chapter by chapter. The different possibilities of the book's usage will be described in this short guide:

- *Short and concise*: Are you looking for a management summary? Then have fun with Chaps. 1 and 2.
- *The languages or the fast Horus user*: Does your interest lie in modeling languages used without wanting to embed these in a comprehensive business process engineering procedure? A question which the typical Horus freeware user might answer with "yes." Then refer to Chap. 3, whereas reading Chap. 2 beforehand might make the entry considerably easier.
- *The method*: Do you already have experience with modeling languages used in business process engineering but want to learn how one can embed these languages in a gradual procedure? You should then start directly with Chap. 4.
- *The meticulous Horus user*: You have downloaded the Horus software and would like to enjoy a solid introduction before starting. Then you should start with Chap. 2 and work up to and including Chap. 4.
- *The professional business process engineer*: The professionals in business process engineering would like to inform themselves quite specifically about different uses and experiences. These readers are referred to Chap. 5.
- *The innovative one*: You understand business process engineering but wish to inform yourself about future topics and current research projects. Then go directly to Chap. 6. If you have further questions regarding secondary information or collaborations, please turn to the Horus Endeavor partners involved.

- *Last, but not least*: You would like to produce a video clip covering the topic of "enterprise routine today." Chapter 1 is then wholeheartedly recommended, asking that you reward us by kindly including a note of thanks in the film trailer.

In this book, we refer to products protected by trademark law and are entitled to their respective owners. These include software products from the following enterprises: Horus software GmbH, Ettlingen, Germany; Oracle Corp., Redwood Shores, CA, USA, and PROMATIS software GmbH, Ettlingen, Germany. Anonymous project examples and excerpts from Horus Knowledge Bases are provided by courtesy of PROMATIS software GmbH, Ettlingen, Germany, and Horus software GmbH, Ettlingen, Germany.

Acknowledgements

An achievement such as this book can never be the result of just a small group of authors. Many contribute without knowing it. The first to be mentioned in this regard are the customers of PROMATIS software GmbH, who have provided the "playing field" for the practice testing of the concepts and products introduced. Thanks also go out to the many colleagues, the scientific and student employees of Horus Endeavor partners that have developed and applied the described in practice. Also, the students who have made valuable contributions to the knowledge of the authors by their active cooperation in lectures, exercises, and training are thanked. During B Semester 2011, the latest version of the text was successfully class-tested at the University of Waikato Management School, Department of Management Systems, courses *MSYS355 E-Business Process Redesign* and *MSYS455 Advanced E-Business Process Redesign* in Hamilton, New Zealand.

A special thanks to the Horus development team, at the very front Yu Li, Johannes Michler, Michael Pergande, and Thomas Schuster, who have implemented the ideas of this book into high-quality software tools. Notable is the high quality and productivity of this collaborative development team. This statement equally applies to Sabine Schwarz, who is responsible for creating and optimizing the numerous illustrations, and to Tanya Quintieri for the laborious translation work.

Ettlingen, Germany	*Frank Schönthaler*
Münster, Germany	*Gottfried Vossen*
Hamilton, New Zealand	
Karlsruhe, Germany	*Andreas Oberweis*
Ettlingen, Germany	*Thomas Karle*

Contents

Chapter 1
Introduction

1.1 Everyday Enterprise Routine: Bad Atmosphere at Confusio Corporation

There is a bustling atmosphere in the headquarters of the globally active Confusio Corporation. Everything seems to be just fine. Yet, there is a bad atmosphere in the precious wood-paneled conference room of the managing director Paul Peppy. Peppy has drummed together his top managers from all important branch offices; a hard and uncompromising crackdown is urgently required! Concerning the topic of the crisis summit, he has intentionally left the participants in the dark. The tension is nearly unbearable, rumors make the round, one whispers about sinking margins and organizational sloppiness. As Peppy finally flings the door open, he vigorously enters the room, and his aggressive eyes fire off ominous flashes in the direction of the sales managers; the culprits have already been identified. With current case studies, which obviously caused his hair to stand on end, Peppy vents his anger and lets the air in grow thin for his sales management. It is hard to believe, but the US sales force has just thrown the German sales team out of the race in a tough bidding competition for a global customer using dumping prices. Team Germany had undercut the Asia team by more than 20% in Malaysia. The Asia team still must be given some credit, as the customer had been classified as a lazy customer in the credit analysis, which the German team missed.

A story from a fairy tale kingdom? Not at all—this is purely case practice! Moreover, it could easily be conveyed to financial institutions, the public sector, foundations, associations, and clubs. However, we want to see how Peppy and his management team tackle the problem. Since the guilty parties were quickly identified, those presumed innocent find a desire to express their opinion and begin to dramatize the cases. The expected impacts on the margins are quickly quantified and are projected to catastrophes with the medium of generalization. The sales managers refer to individual cases and vow improvement. The discussion becomes emotional, and threatens to escalate, when Peppy finally steps in and asks Fritz Cunning, who is moving about in his seat uneasily, to structure the problem.

F. Schönthaler et al., *Business Processes for Business Communities*,
DOI 10.1007/978-3-642-24791-0_1, © Springer-Verlag Berlin Heidelberg 2012

1.1.1   Structuring the Problem

Cunning meets his bosses' expectations. With the help of pin boards and flipcharts, he at first starts to summarize and to structure the discussion points in a mind map. He lists arguments, objectives, strengths, and weaknesses in structure trees. Moreover, Fritz Cunning succeeds par excellence with what no one had expected: He takes the edge out of the discussion and eliminates opposition by actively engaging all those present into his analysis, creating transparency. Moreover, his informal documentation techniques provide him with good services, since they are simple and understandable and demand little abstraction capabilities from the participants while developing a high visualization power. Peppy benevolently looks at the results of his "secret weapon" Cunning. It is more than clear that the locally optimal bidding process failed in the global context and a consequent reengineering must take place. However, what must the new process look like for the proposal system? In addition, how shall it be put into practice quickly and economically?

1.1.2   The Solution

All eyes are on Fritz Cunning, who once again has the advice and the proper tools prepared. He relies on the technique of *Petri nets*, and with that he outlines the essential features of the previous bidding procedure. Using this easy-to-understand graphical model, he points to the weaknesses of the current process. By creating a link to the documents that were jointly prepared during the previous informal analysis, he easily manages to turn all the attendees into *participants* of this creative engineering approach. Together, the idea of globalizing the bidding process is developed and is additionally modeled in a Petri net.

And as usual, the overall satisfaction and acceptance quite quickly gives way to skepticism. Of course, the new process seems convincing, someone throws in, but the devil is in the details. Cunning refutes this argument because with Petri nets, he has selected a technique that enables him to *refine* rough models arbitrarily to work out the relevant details. The chief information officer points out that so much effort would be put into a model that could potentially prove to be useless for future IT implementation. Cunning counters with the *automated implementation* of Petri nets into executable workflows and services. Somebody wants to know whether the new business process also will be able to cope with the seasonally conditional load peaks or if additional staff will become necessary. Cunning is pleased about this question, because he can play out the essential strength of his Petri net approach, and promises to resolve these questions using a *simulation study* and thus to provide quantitative results and to visualize the model directly.

Peppy smiles contentedly, however secretly worried about whether the new bidding procedure will really be economic, i.e., if the service quality valued by the customers will be met or even surpassed and if cost savings will be possible. Prudent Cunning anticipates his bosses' worries and can help here as well. By means of static analysis and dynamic simulation, he is able to directly show costs and benefits in his Petri nets and offer solid forecasts for the profitability of the future business process.

1.1.3 What It Is All About

At this point, we leave the wood-paneled meeting room where the bad atmosphere is no longer dominant. This small scene makes the importance of using effective documentation and visualization techniques clear and that it is also important to complement it with formal modeling instruments in organizational work. The requirements placed on such instruments in terms of documentation requirements, visualization, analysis, and simulation are fulfilled only when powerful software tools are used. Petri nets offer the ideal platform for tool support and the scientific maturity with their approved mathematical foundations for wide practical use.

1.2 Modeling Languages and Methods

In a globalized world, business processes increasingly form the crux of any organization. Why is this so? Well, the explanation is comparatively simple, if one considers that any change in an organization will be accompanied by changes inseparable with its business processes. Changes in the global market are common for the daily agenda: Companies are increasingly forced to adapt to new customers, competitors, and business partners. Competitive edges are achieved more frequently not by better products, but by efficient and cost-effective processes. In short, business processes have developed into an additional factor of production.

1.2.1 Language of the Business Community

Given this background, it is no surprise that of all the professionals and managers today, but also the IT staff, suppliers, and sometimes even the customers of a company—we collectively call this the *business community*—are expected to have a good look at *business processes*. Together, they contribute to the design, analysis, documentation, execution, and further development of business processes. Of course, this only succeeds if an efficient communication is possible. This requires that the same language is used within the entire business community and that time-consuming and error-prone translation operations are omitted. However, what does this look like in practice? Obscurities, contradictions, misunderstandings, and omissions in communication are common. Each interest group in the business community maintains its group-specific perspective on a business process: The management focuses on business performance indicators, business professionals have their business applications and processes in mind, and IT professionals think in software and hardware structures. It is clear that communication problems are inevitable. In many organizations, one tries to remedy this with modeling experts who "translate" the collected business requirements into process requirements, summarizing these in vast and highly complex models. Such an approach gives the appearance of professionalism and efficiency, and in fact, such "model monsters" are often given the stamp of approval by the entire business community forming the basis of organizational change. Many community members recognize the implications of the "model monsters" at a point far too late when they have to live with the organizational changes.

Figure 1.1 shows an alternative approach that is based on the use of a common modeling language. This language is understood and (ideally) "spoken" fluently by all members of the business community involved. This means that an explicit translation of the communication processes will not be necessary, and the abstraction of group-specific perspectives as well as structuring of the contents conveyed can be carried out individually by everyone involved.

Which prerequisites are necessary for such a universal modeling language? First, it must be easy to learn and can be mastered by inexperienced users quickly and reliably. The language must provide all technically relevant aspects of a business process in detail. All this is possible only if the language has a simple syntax, which requires a minimum number of language elements, and clearly defined semantics that distinctly govern the use and interpretation of the elements.

When we apply these criteria to modeling languages used in common practice, it is immediately clear why they can only be used by "experts": With a variety of modeling elements—mostly "spiced up" with pictographs (recognition effects should suggest simplicity and create an understanding)—it is attempted to convey

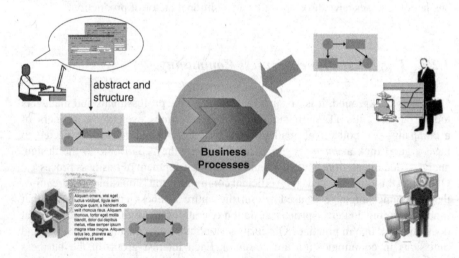

Fig. 1.1 A common language as a prerequisite for communication

a clear view of reality in every conceivable application field. This proliferation of syntax will be paid for with a strikingly vague definition of semantics.

A look into the related field of data modeling shows that this is the wrong path. There, a mathematically sound model has established itself as an industry standard with the relational database model by Ted Codd and the accompanying query language SQL with a syntactically simple language. Petri nets also have these "success characteristics": Simple syntax with clean mathematically defined semantics, which include not only a clear interpretation of model elements but also dynamic characteristics in terms of state transitions. Petri nets therefore offer diverse possibilities for static analysis and dynamic simulation. An informal introduction to Petri nets can be found in Chap. 3.

1.2.2 Modeling Methods

Simplicity of use combined with various fields of application—these strengths of Petri nets can then develop best when they are integrated in a proven modeling method. The method provides for when Petri nets are used in a particular way. In addition, it regulates when and how analysis and simulation are to be used and which results can be obtained there from. A specific method for working with Petri nets in business communities is presented in Chap. 4 of this book.

1.3 Tools for Business Communities

Efficient work with Petri nets and the application of relevant methods are inconceivable without software tool support. Tools ensure compliance with the syntactic rules, support methodical steps, and take over tasks of the administration, documentation, and use of content created.

1.3.1 Market Development

Meanwhile, the history of the model-based design of business processes reaches back to more than 20 years. After the first tentative beginnings within the context of computer-aided software engineering tools (CASE), business process modeling has experienced its first high point in the context of the introduction of standard business application software (SAP, Oracle Applications, PeopleSoft, Baan, etc.). Besides high-end tools such as ADONIS, ARIS, Bonaparte, Casewise, and INCOME, low-end tools increasingly appeared on the market as well, which had evolved from simple drawing programs, such as Visio and iGrafx. Today we are experiencing a second high point, whose drivers are undoubtedly the subjects of *business process management* (BPM), *model-driven development* (MDD), and *service-oriented architecture* (SOA). A current market observation shows that virtually every application software and middleware supplier has at least one process modeling tool to offer.

It quickly becomes clear upon closer inspection, however, that the tools are only conditionally suitable for use in business communities. They require a high level of training and force users into a procedure that is not based on their needs but to the restrictions of the tool. In most cases, the complexity is too high (e.g., a multitude of model types in ARIS), or the limited abstraction possibilities force users excessively at the implementation level (e.g., modeling with BPMN) and prevent the all-important creative modeling processes. For the tools' "retrieval of honor," it must be noted, however, that they were created at a time in which the needs of a participation of whole business communities in the development of business processes were not yet recognized, and the technical possibilities for effective community work (keyword: Web 2.0) were not yet available.

1.3.2   Horus: Business Processes for Business Communities

As a result of many years of research at the Institute for Applied Computer Science and Formal Description Methods (AIFB) of the Karlsruhe Institute of Technology (KIT) and the Karlsruhe Research Center for Computer Science (FZI) in collaboration with industrial partner PROMATIS software GmbH, a whole new generation of tools to support the entire life cycle of business processes has emerged under the name of *Horus*.[1] The main research objective was to enable and promote the participation and interaction of all members of a business community. For this, the technical possibilities that have become available in the socialization of the Web were exhausted. Horus is based on the operation of the community, without disturbing their processes, and is thus manageable without extensive training. The most important Horus components are briefly outlined.

1.3.2.1   Petri Net Platform

Horus provides a platform for modeling, analysis, and simulation with Petri nets. It features simplicity of use and runs on all common operating systems and portable devices. As a special net variant, *XML nets* are supported. The platform is free and available for all business communities as well as for teaching and research (Horus

---

[1]Horus—the "Distant One"—is one of the most important gods in Egyptian mythology. As a falcon, he rises into the air and stretches his wings as heaven over the earth; the sun and moon are his eyes.

freeware). A professional distribution (Horus Enterprise) may also be purchased from Horus software GmbH, for which a support contract can be closed.

1.3.2.2   Content and Community

In the free platform, ready-made models are included as content in order to facilitate the first steps with Horus. In addition, communities can be established within Intranet and Internet business communities that support the exchange of models as well as the collaborative work within the community. Complete business process models are offered by Horus software GmbH.

1.3.2.3   Application Fields

Horus covers the complete life cycle of a business process, from the initial idea to the design up to the use and maintenance of the process. It supports administrative and analytical as well as creative tasks. Horus can be embedded seamlessly in a custom-designed infrastructure through web service and XML interfaces, which are included in the professional distribution.

This will provide numerous new applications, ranging from the restructuring of the company (business reengineering) to the introduction of standard business application software and building service-oriented architecture up to interactive methods of organizational learning.

1.4   Objectives and Structure of This Book

Many books have been written in recent years on business processes. Some treat the subject in a theoretical manner and others more through a practical point of view. This book has arisen out of the idea of combining an easy-to-understand presentation of the topic containing practical examples and application guides, combining a clean introduction into the formal basics. This book is suitable as a tool for practitioners and as a basis for practical courses at universities. A practical approach is also formed by the representation of concepts and methods of using the software tool Horus. Horus is also understood as a typical representative of the Petri net tools, so that the book is a valuable companion also for non-Horus users.

The book requires no particular formal knowledge as a prerequisite. Knowledge of operational processes and structures, however, makes comprehension and understanding easier. The book is aimed at professionals and business executives as well as teachers and students. Business disciplines are addressed as well as computer science and engineering.

The book captivates the reader in Chap. 2, at first into a real business environment. There, the most important fundamentals of model-based business process engineering are described informally with numerous practical examples. Building on this, Chap. 3 describes the relevant concepts and modeling languages and develops a coherent framework for business process modeling. Chapter 4 shows an integrated approach, the *Horus method*, to model-based business process engineering. The starting point builds a strategy analysis that embeds the business processes in a complete company context. In Chap. 5, concrete practice examples are described. The book closes in Chap. 6 with a look into the future of business process engineering.

1.5   Bibliographical Notes and Web Links

Dealing with business processes, their analysis and improvement goes back to Hammer and Champy (1993), among others. In the 1990s, the issue was considered particularly in the context of workflow management, see Van der Aalst and Van Hee (2004). In the meantime, the literature on business process modeling varies between extensive and confusing, so we refer our readers at this point only to Becker et al. (2011), Scheer (2000a,b), Davis (2001), and Weske (2007). Those who prefer an introduction to the subject in novel form vs. the dry textbook version, Grosskopf et al. (2009) is recommended.

The following links refer to general web pages covering the topic of business process models or business process modeling and management:

- Business Process Management Initiative: www.bpmi.org
- Business Process Modeling Forum: www.bpmodeling.com/
- Business Process Trends: www.bptrends.com/
- Petri Nets World: www.informatik.uni-hamburg.de/TGI/PetriNets

The following links give examples of systems for business process modeling to which more information is available on the Web; this list is not complete:

- ARIS Express by Software AG: www.ariscommunity.com/aris-express
- bflow Toolbox (Open Source): www.bflow.org/
- Horus by Horus software GmbH: www.horus.biz/en.html
- Signavio Process Editor by Signavio GmbH: www.signavio.com/en.html
- TIBCO Business Studio by TIBCO Software Inc.: developer.tibco.com

Chapter 2
Practical Introduction to Business Process Engineering

The design of business processes is not a new discipline but is essentially as old as the creation of products and labor services. Over time, the originally purely experiential approach has been augmented by an engineering component so that one speaks today of *business process engineering*. This circumscribes the design and layout, the analysis, improvement, optimization as well as the documentation of operational activities and their basic conditions. This is done, in practice, far too often only with the help of informal tools—with natural language text, including tables and graphics, for example. The simple comprehensibility often is paid for with inconsistencies and omissions in the resulting process descriptions. The consequences are dangerous as well as costly quality problems in the practical implementation of such processes. The remedy is a formal graphical modeling technique. This will provide significant quality improvements in business process engineering and the subsequent process of implementation.

This chapter takes a practical approach to model-based engineering of business processes. It deliberately abstracts from modeling details and does so without the embedding into an overall methodological context. To this end, references are made to Chap. 3 and notably Chap. 4 of this book.

2.1 The Task

For a practical introduction to business process engineering, we have selected a typical scenario from the sales area: Complex products that require explanation are distributed, which generally have a multistep sales cycle. Business customers will be processed exclusively and will include both existing as well as prospective customers, where an active business relationship has not yet been established. The distribution process is executed by a sales team, which maintains close intensive contacts in different areas and levels of the target customer.

The exact objective that business process engineering will follow is irrelevant in this introductory chapter. It is important to understand how real-world relationships

F. Schönthaler et al., *Business Processes for Business Communities*,
DOI 10.1007/978-3-642-24791-0_2, © Springer-Verlag Berlin Heidelberg 2012

are acquired, analyzed, and illustrated in a business model. This model is then used for a visualization of business processes, and it allows a particularly efficient and effective form of communication when technical requirements of the process are involved. Equally important is the perception that a mapping of real-world situations and contexts into a model with clearly defined syntax and semantics represents much more than a simple collection and listing of requirements: The rules of the model force an analysis of the requirements and essentially pushes the modeler onto errors, omissions, inconsistencies, redundancies, and unnecessary operations.

2.2   Analysis and Modeling of Processes

The first question that must be answered in the context of business process engineering sounds quite trivial: "How to start?" "With the procedures, of course!" As obviously correct as this answer is—business primarily thinks in procedures— the start is often initiated with the organization structure. Why so? Apparently, such a start inevitably leads to business processes that align themselves to the organization structure and not to the business needs that are reflected directly in the procedures. The reasons for the prioritizing of structural organization issues can, in many cases, be found in the defense and the expansion of spheres of power. Our urgent recommendation is therefore to focus in a first step on the procedures and to consciously abstract from the organization structure. Only when the analysis of the procedures is freed from the shackles of the organizational structure can genuine process improvements and innovations be expected.

2.2.1   Process Modeling with Petri Nets

Let us focus on the procedures of the sales process. Essentially, the business procedures consist of a sequence of activities and of an associated object flow. Activities can be of the manual type or be partially automated by using information and communication technologies. Objects for us are documents, data, knowledge, or even short messages or control signals. Even real goods (products, raw materials and supplies, etc.) are interpreted as objects.

The first task is to portray the procedures of the considered distribution process in a formal, graphical model. For this, we use so-called *XML nets*, a special form of Petri nets. Petri nets, named after German mathematician Carl Adam Petri, have proven to be successful for many years in the modeling of dynamic systems. Petri nets are impressive in business process modeling due to the simplicity of the graphical presentation in connection with their expressive power and performance. This is especially true for XML nets. A high model precision is achieved and the operational semantics allows formal analysis and dynamic simulations. The central characteristic of XML nets is that objects are described in *XML* (short for *Extensible*

Markup Language). The use of the linguistic framework XML—now an industry standard in the electronic processing of documents and of business processes—allows a detailed collection of object structures or a convenient formulation of design principles for the activities and additionally opens up interesting new application fields.

Modeling is no easy task even for the relatively simple sales process: Activities and object flows must be extracted from unstructured basic information of the business that is then to be structured and portrayed in the model. The *Horus method* described in Chap. 4 offers practice-proven approaches in this regard. Figure 2.1 shows an overview of the sales process procedures, here represented as a Petri net. As is common practice, the process is given a name, which allows conclusions regarding input and output objects of the process—here `Sales Contact-to-Order`. This means that the process starts with a sales contact, and includes a series of activities and necessary object flows, and ultimately generates an order.

The Petri net of the distribution procedure describes the first step of a prequalified sales contact and the subsequent transition to a qualified sales contact (`Lead`). Simultaneously, an entry is made in the customer master data. In addition to the *activities* represented as rectangles, *object stores* (circles) are contained within the net, from which activities take objects according to the direction of the arrow (e.g., `Sales contact`) or where activities store objects (e.g., `Lead` and `Customer master data`), whereby in this network, the use of XML or XML nets cannot yet be recognized (this will become clear later in this chapter).

Leads are further qualified into the cultivation of contacts, which is reflected in an updating of the customer master data. The goal is to identify real sales

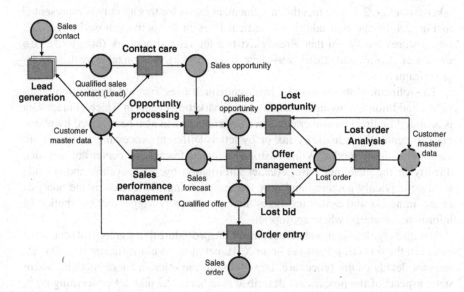

Fig. 2.1 Modeling a sales process as a Petri net

opportunities, which are then intensively processed to ultimately lead to an offer. Ideally, the offer will lead to a customer order. With the sales process, failures are also considered: Lost sales opportunities and lost bids will be combined in the object store Lost order and then subjected to a Lost order analysis. This analysis is a read-only access of the customer master data, which is represented by a simple connection without arrowheads. Object store Customer master data is represented in the net twice, while the copy is shown dashed. In addition to the central sales procedure, a sales performance management activity is also taken into account. This activity analyzes the sales forecast that includes information regarding the content and status of current offers.

2.2.2   Refinement of the Process Model

An analysis of the overview net shown in Fig. 2.1 quickly shows that many details must deliberately be abstracted from. A number of questions arise which can be viewed as an advantage of modeling: How, by whom, and in what temporal sequence does contact care take place, and how does a sales opportunity ultimately develop from a sales contact? Also behind the offer management, represented in the network as simple box only, hides a demanding process with detailed activities, object flows, and rules which the output object store Qualified offer already leads to assume. These and similar questions can be answered if the activities of the network are refined even again by own networks. In technology, one would speak of an exploded view.

Figure 2.2 exemplarily shows the refined lead generation activity of the network taken from Fig. 2.1. The fact that a refinement exists for this activity is represented in Fig. 2.1 by the two additional vertical lines in the activity box. In Fig. 2.2, object stores are shown that already exist in the refined network (herein: Sales contact, Lead, and Customer master data), recognizable by the rectangular frame.

The refinement shows that the lead acquisition uses assorted distribution channels: In addition to playing an active part in marketing events in which contact data is acquired in direct customer contact, sales contacts can also be received by phone via call center, by e-mail, by fax or by letter. Different processing scenarios are identifiable in the model: While customer contacts from a call center are recorded directly in the customer base, contact information by mail, events, and e-mails must be explicitly gathered and may require scanning. Of interest is the analysis of incoming fax and e-mail messages that automatically trigger the distribution of information material where appropriate.

It is already clear in this short account of the procedure that a graphical procedure model in the form of a Petri net or an XML net alone is not sufficient to define all relevant details of the procedure. In addition to the referencing of models, where static aspects of the process are described (see Sects. 2.3 and 2.4 concerning this), short textual descriptions are added to the graphical elements. It is important that

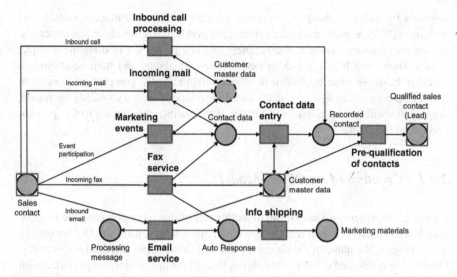

Fig. 2.2 Refinement of activity `Lead generation`

these descriptions be formulated in a clearly understandable language with diligent use of common technical vocabulary.

Short and concise sentences are preferred; bullet lists have also proven to be effective. It is important that what is already shown in the graphic not be repeated in the description and that additional information be given to supplement the graphical model and ease its understanding. As a rule of thumb, textual descriptions should not exceed half a regular page size. Should this amount not suffice, a further model refinement should be considered. Having proven themselves in practice are concrete sample documents, screen shots, or informal sketches that are assigned the formal elements and considerably promote the understanding of the model. This is in addition to all submodels, by the way.

2.3 Business Objects and Object Flows

The procedure model, with its activities and object flows, constitutes the central reference point of a business process model. And because the business legitimately places the procedures in the forefront of the analysis, many business process engineering projects are limited to the procedure analysis in practice. However, *our* goal is to consider *all* relevant aspects of the business process. Only by these means can we be certain to have analyzed and included the process as a whole. We therefore turn next to the *business objects* on which the procedures of the process operate.

Business objects are produced, read, modified, and consumed by activities of the business process (also known as the "CRUD cycle" for *Create, Read, Update, Destroy* operations). This may be in the form of not only documents (contracts, business forms, etc.), database objects (customer master or transaction data), text messages (SMS, e-mail, etc.) but also tangible goods like products or raw materials. In our introductory example, the business objects are shown in a business object model. Business objects are described by their attributes and their relationships to other business objects. Business objects are generally complex and are then formed by combining several objects and their relations with a so-called aggregate. Aggregates will not be considered further at this point; please refer to Chap. 3 for additional information.

2.3.1 Creation of an Object Model

Figure 2.3 represents a view of the object model of our sales process. The objects, which are represented as a rectangle with rounded edges, form the framework. In the rectangles, the name of the object is indicated in the upper text field respectively. Objects are connected to each other through relationships, which are provided with a respective name. In the sample model, a customer places a customer orders.

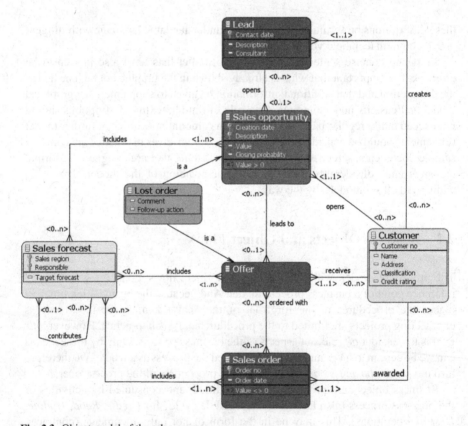

Fig. 2.3 Object model of the sales process

For relationships, cardinalities define how many objects of an associated object type are related at least and at most. For the relation between Customer and Sales order, the cardinality indicates $< 0 \ldots n >$ on the part of the customer, that either none or any number of customer orders exist. The "crow's foot" at the other end of the relation represents this cardinality graphically. Since a sales order is assigned to exactly one customer, the cardinality finds itself there $< 1 \ldots 1 >$ with a simple line connection in the direction of the customer.

Key attributes are specified for the objects, respectively e.g., the customer number for the customer), and *descriptive attributes* (e.g., for the customer the attributes name, address, classification, and credit rating). To keep the efforts in model creation within a justifiable frame, one normally confines oneself to such attributes that are indispensable to the comprehension of the object, (or to the required formal specification of execution rules in the XML net). Therefore, it is not atypical that the specification of attributes is also omitted, as is the case in the object Offer. Simple *integrity constraints*, which locally refer to the object, are specified directly at the object. In the example of Sales order, it is required that the order value is not equal to zero.

The graphic object model shows an especially interesting model fragment in the middle: Represented is the life cycle of a customer contact (Lead), that ideally opens a sales opportunity (consider the cardinality $< 0 \ldots n >$, that shows that leads also exist that have not (yet) led to a sales opportunity). From a sales opportunity (cardinality $< 0 \ldots 1 >$ implies that there are Sales opportunities without a previous Lead) either none, one or more sales can be the result (cardinality $< 0 \ldots n >$) and from that the resulting corresponding sales orders. Such a "life-cycle model" is quite frequent in practice. Undoubtedly, it underlines with its relationships and cardinalities the value of an object model. It also makes clear that a consideration of the object model allows drawing conclusions as to the correctness and completeness of the business procedures, which is of high value in quality management.

Recursive relationships can be portrayed elegantly as well, as this can be seen by the example of the sales forecast: Sales regions appear to be arranged in a hierarchical structure so that the sales forecast of one region contains the sales forecasts of the subordinate regions.

Also interesting is the use of *specializations* (a.k.a. *Is-A relationships*), as can be seen with the Lost order example. Lost orders are spoken of in connection with lost sales opportunities or offers. In addition, an inheritance of properties through the differentiation of a special object (keys, attributes, integrity constraints, relationships) to the parent object follows, that is—against the arrow direction—from the Offer on the Lost order.

2.3.2   Typing of Objects

Once the business objects in the object model of the business process are defined, it is recommended to establish a connection to the procedure model: With the

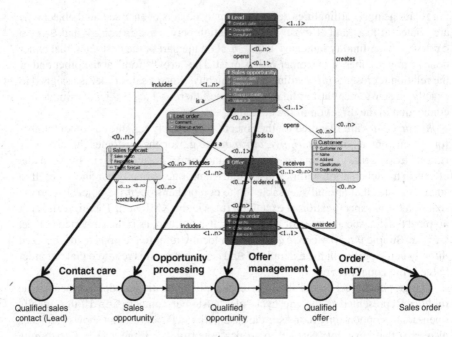

Fig. 2.4 Typing of the object stores in the XML net

allocation of object types to object stores, the objects of the procedure model can be typed in a simple manner. The objects of the object model are formally assigned to the object stores of the XML nets. The interpretation therefore allows statements about the structure and the features of the objects deposited in the object stores. Furthermore, it will be possible to define transition rules in the activities, which access object contents. Thus, attributes of input objects can be compared with another, or it can be determined how the attribute value of an output object is calculated from attributes of the input objects.

Figure 2.4 shows a part of the procedure model from Fig. 2.1 together with the object model in Fig. 2.3. Arrows point from the object stores to the objects, where the type of the corresponding objects is specified. Key and descriptive attributes of the objects are defined that way. In addition, the integrity constraints will ensure that in the object store `Sales order` only orders with a contract value not equal to zero may be stored.

2.4   Process-Oriented Organization Structures

The procedure model in the form of XML nets and the object model already represent the framework of a business process model. Referencing the models offers an ideal starting point for static quality analysis. On this basis, one can now set up an organization structure that aims strictly at the business processes. In practice, when designing organization structures, aspects are significant which cannot be derived from the business process model: company strategy, career paths, skills and experience of personnel, labor costs, labor law issues, and such. Of which is to be abstracted at this point.

An *organization chart* is shown in Fig. 2.5, which orientates itself at the viewed sales process. The business area is divided into three sales regions: Germany, Europe/Middle East/Africa (EMEA), and the rest of the world (RoW). The operational functions are combined in the sales office. The interaction center takes care of the contact-to-lead process, that is, the generation, collection, primary processing and prequalification of sales leads. The processing of sales opportunities, the quote management, and the extraction of the orders—that is, the lead-to-order process—lies in the responsibility of the sales regions. These are supported by the sales service suspended within the office staff and the customer order entry. While the interaction center, order entry, and sales service are disciplinarily assigned to the sales office, a reporting line to sales Germany still exists—as indicated by the dotted lines. This is not atypical if one wants to avoid dangerous "back office silos." A reporting channel into a market-focused organizational unit often provides a strongly improved market orientation.

At this point we will leave our introductory example. The aim was to convey an impression of the opportunities arising from model-based business process engineering. In the following chapters, the modeling languages used are dealt with in detail and embedded in a general methodological context.

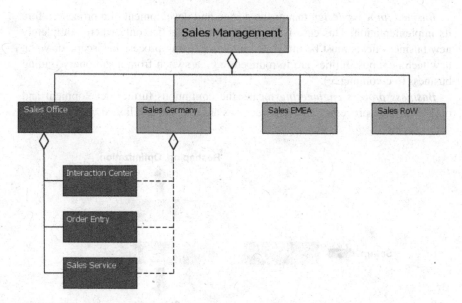

Fig. 2.5 Organization structure of the sales area

2.5   Holistic Business Process Management

Business process management is an important constituent of a lasting recipe for success in many successful and future-oriented companies, as is the case in our example. The different aspects of the business processes relevant for the companies are fully described, documented, and made transparent for all persons involved, so that they may adequately become a part of the process. In addition to a full documentation, the goal of business process management is an improvement or optimization of processes. This may occur under different objectives. In principle, there are numerous possible goals or several continuous activities of business process management as represented in Fig. 2.6:

- *Design*: Business process management is set up for the first time and introduced. The processes of the companies in question are subjected to a design.
- *Engineering*: Designed processes are implemented and made available for execution. An efficient resource use is important, furthermore an adequate connection of process, object, and organization models.
- *Monitoring*: Existing and preestablished business processes are subject to continuous monitoring to identify and remove bottlenecks in processes or resource allocation. The management of the business processes is improving constantly; this can be done continuously or at specific time intervals. The goal is a continuous optimization of the current operations of existing processes.
- *Reengineering*: An established process management is redesigned or optimized partly or completely because of changed organizational conditions.

Business process design means the design and development of a process before its implementation. This case is usually found in practice only where completely new business fields must be integrated into an existing process landscape or when new technical possibilities are introduced (e.g., a switch from a stationary trading business to e-commerce).

Business process engineering means the continuous further development and optimization of processes. Proven processes are retained and linked with improved

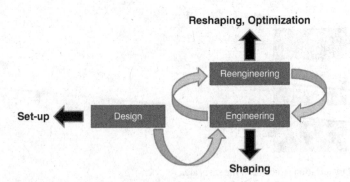

Fig. 2.6 Objectives of business process management

or partially redesigned processes. The changes may not be drastic, they take place gradually. For one, the risk that a transformation always brings with it is reduced and the acceptance on the other hand is improved. A prerequisite for this evolutionary form of business process development is a permanent monitoring. Only then, weaknesses can be identified and the impact of the changes displayed and analyzed.

All these objectives require a precise definition of the business processes as well as a consistent documentation, which can be achieved by adequate modeling.

The original method introduced by Hammer and Champy in 1993 for *business process reengineering* (BPR) relies on a radical redesign of the existing process landscape. For best results, all processes will be newly developed. Proven processes, however, remain unconsidered. Because of the serious changes, which a radical change generally causes, the model could not gain acceptance in "pure form" in operational practice. A redesign, on the other hand, of entire subareas of a company can and will be carried out.

Generally accepted nowadays is *holistic business process management*, which on the one hand takes the indicated aspects of the procedure modeling, object modeling as well as organization modeling already indicated here into consideration and on the other hand takes the business view (abstracting from processes) as well as the service view (implementing processes and their constituents) into account; this is indicated in Fig. 2.7.

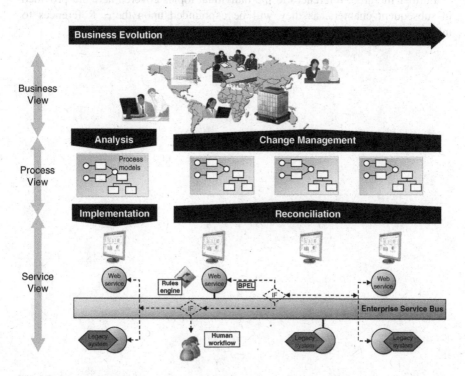

Fig. 2.7 Integrated business process management

For modeling and an analysis of business processes, as already mentioned, several methods can be used, one of which is described more detailed in Chap. 4. Let it be mentioned at this point that either top-down, from top to bottom (method of increasing specialization), or bottom-up, that is from the bottom to the top (method of increasing abstraction), can be used. Which approach (or a combination) is chosen depends on specific circumstances; however, a top-down approach is to be preferred in most cases.

2.6   Bibliographic Notes

Clear and understandable introductions to process modeling may be found in, among others, Dutton (1993) and Weske (2007), case studies also in Scheer (2000a, b). An introduction to Petri nets is given by Reisig (2011), one to XML by Vonhoegen (2009).

The object model considered here is obviously closely related to the Entity Relationship Model (ERM) originally proposed by Chen (1976): The ERM uses not only double-digit relationships, as those in our introductory example are sufficient (see Fig. 2.3).

Further literature references to the individual topics covered here are provided in subsequent chapters, as they will be expounded upon there. References to information on the Web, also provided in Chap. 1, are valid.

Chapter 3
Concepts and Modeling Languages

In this chapter, the concepts and modeling languages are introduced which are
required for modeling, particularly of processes, objects, and organization structures in the remainder of this book. Initially, there is a brief explanation of the
necessity and the motivation behind modeling. As a concrete modeling language
for processes, Petri nets are introduced. The representation is rounded off by
complementing pure process modeling with object modeling as well as with
organization modeling.

In the scenario of the sales area discussed in Chap. 2, it was first necessary to
map one or several procedures; these were designed in a crude manner in a first
step and were subsequently refined. Business objects were eventually modeled and
assigned to the procedure structures, and the accompanying organization structure
was reviewed. Particularly, the first two aspects, the procedure modeling as well as
object modeling, will be examined more closely in this chapter. The concepts used
will be introduced later in this chapter.

Firstly, the general objective is to represent and illustrate the procedures of an
enterprise in appropriate models; initially, the different views in business process
modeling will be discussed in Sect. 3.2. The goal is also to conduct a detailed
analysis of models created in this way to identify potential improvements. Through
the use of Petri nets (Sect. 3.3), it is additionally possible to simulate procedures in
process models, in order to arrive at efficiency statements prior to their execution
within the enterprise. In addition to pure process modeling, business objects are
also described and modeled, which will be created, read, modified, or destroyed by
processes or single activities; this occurs in Sect. 3.4. Finally, the organization of an
enterprise as a whole will be considered in the modeling (Sect. 3.5).

F. Schönthaler et al., *Business Processes for Business Communities*,   21
DOI 10.1007/978-3-642-24791-0_3, © Springer-Verlag Berlin Heidelberg 2012

3.1 Introduction

3.1.1 Modeling

In many areas of everyday life, models play an important role. Examples of models are building plans, knitting patterns, weather maps, timetables, city maps, other maps, technical drawings, etc. Models are simplified descriptions of certain facts of the real world or an imaginary world, with which one pursues a certain goal. The city map, for example, allows for orientation in a city or to find a particular street or a particular building. Models *abstract* from such aspects which are not required to achieve the modeling objective; for example, information about persons living in the buildings or information about the height of buildings cannot be found on a city map. Models are abstractions or reductions of reality, not exact copies or reproductions. Models can describe with varying degrees of accuracy and from certain perspectives.

Different goals are pursued with models. In art, for example, the term *model* is used in the sense of an exemplar, which is depicted more or less accurately in a work of art. Knitting patterns also serve as a template, for knitting sweaters for example. Models play an important role in information technology. Information technology builds systems to solve real-world problems. In this regard, models represent communication media in the broadest sense.

A modeling goal in information technology may be:

- The analysis of a particular issue at an abstract level, such as the behavior of an electronic circuit; the models used here are Boolean functions.
- Development of algorithmic solutions for a given problem. As an example, think of building a timetable for examinations in a department; graphs, for example, in which so-called maximum sets of independent nodes are sought after, serve as a model here.
- Evidence of desirable or undesirable properties before building a system.
- Communications support between different groups of people involved in a development, such as between developers and users, and between business analysts and programmers.
- Planning the use of resources during system runtime.
- Documentation of a system in terms of a user manual.
- Depiction of a system as a basis for maintenance.

There are different languages for modeling different aspects of a system. The spectrum of the possible languages reaches from mathematically formal notations or notations of (propositional or predicate) logic to graphical languages (as we will use here to describe processes or objects) as well as programming languages like Java or C# up to colloquial forms of expression. In the following, for modeling tasks of interest, special Petri nets, so-called *XML nets*, will be used to model processes, as these nets possess a well-defined semantics, yet at the same time allow, by their graphic representation, for an intuitive and comprehensive modeling and a precise specification of the underlying data structure.

3.1.2 Simulation

In many cases, desirable investigations in the real world are not possible to be executed with real systems (e.g., how a machine behaves in a certain error situation. Do the individual components work together correctly? Can the workload that the system supports be scaled appropriately?), whether for cost-efficiency reasons or, for example, because a trial-and-error run in reality poses unacceptable risks to the environment (e.g., testing an aircraft control system in an actual flying aircraft). *Simulation* helps in such a situation, that is, the systematic trial and error based on a model, known as the *simulation model*, and based on certain scenarios which can be described via an appropriate parameterization of the simulation model.

In an ideal situation, the knowledge gained from a simulation can be transferred to the real system immediately. The quality of the simulation is dependent on the quality of the model, that is, on the question how well the model describes the respective reality. In fact, simulation only allows proof of nonfulfillment of model characteristics of the type "system always behaves like this ...," but not the proof of the fulfillment of such statements. Simulation therefore always considers only certain situations: How does a model behave for a given initial state with given environmental conditions? Because a simulation model must abstract from certain details of the real system, contingent on complexity, the result of a simulation also differs more or less from the corresponding behavior of the real system. For complexity reasons, therefore, no statements are possible of the type: "The model always responds as intended." In the worst case, an infinite number of simulation runs would be required.

Simulation is particularly interesting for process modeling, since it allows running through specific process flows without having already carried out an implementation of these particular flows. Here, another particular advantage of the choice of Petri nets as a modeling tool will turn up, namely the fact that they can be executed in a simulative manner. In the further course of this book, we will illustrate this aspect; as we shall see, a simulation of process models is supported by Horus effectively and efficiently.

3.1.3 Analysis

Analysis describes the systematic, often algorithmic examination of a model for determining properties of a system, a process, or another object under consideration. The properties of a model are actually provable by adequate analysis. The transferability of analytical results to a real system is also dependent on the quality of the model used.

For complexity reasons, however, an analysis is often not applicable, or only applicable to small systems or for only some part of the possible initial conditions, or possible environmental conditions. Moreover, not all properties of a system are analyzable or provable in this way. The usability of a system, for example, cannot be analyzed in this sense since it cannot be described precisely (i.e., mathematically). Analysis, however, presupposes the precise description of the respective system properties in a model.

In practice, analytical and simulative examinations of models complement each other. Analysis is useful for certain system components and system features, particularly critically assessed ones. Simulation comes into question for other characteristics. These aspects will be illustrated later in this chapter for process modeling.

3.1.4   Monitoring

Monitoring is the supervision of processes and systems. For example, a database administrator supervises one or more database systems with regard to their performance. If bottlenecks occur, for instance because the rate of released transactions per time interval falls below a certain limit, the administrator can intervene, for example, by enlarging the lock table.

Similar activities are often found in information technology systems and their applications. Here, we are interested in the aspect of monitoring processes under execution. Again, performance bottlenecks can occur, which often can be explained by design decisions which were made during the modeling phase and which have not appeared during a simulation. Furthermore, a situation can appear at the runtime of processes, which was or could not be foreseen during the modeling phase. Both situations must be adequately addressed, either by intervening during the execution of a current process instance, or by modification of the underlying process model.

Over time, monitoring will thus lead to an *evolution* of process models in order to match current technical requirements on the one hand and to adapt to other necessary changes in process logic on the other.

Overall, this brief discussion shows that, on the one hand, a modeling and its resulting model should *represent* a specific situation or process. On the other hand, this ideally occurs in a manner that allows assertions or statements about the modeled circumstances or process in the form of a *simulation*, furthermore allowing *analysis* as well as *monitoring* (compare also Fig. 2.6). As will be seen in the further course of our presentation, this is true of Petri nets in general and of XML nets in particular, so that these are particularly suitable for business process modeling.

3.2   Business Process Modeling Views

Processes occur in daily life in different contexts and meanings, such as a chemical process, a trial in front of a court, or the execution process of a computer program. Here, we would like to restrict the attention to processes that are business processes.

The contemplation of business processes goes back to the early 1990s and to Michael Hammer, at that time a professor at the MIT Sloan School of Management, and James Champy, a lawyer and business consultant, who released their famous book *Reengineering the Corporation: A Manifesto for Business Revolution* back in 1993. It was already then when *Publishers Weekly* wrote:

> Management consultants Hammer and Champy thoughtfully critique the management procedures of American business and offer a promising prescription in this invigorating study. "It is no longer necessary or desirable for companies to organize their work around Adam Smith's division of labor," they state, arguing that task-oriented jobs are becoming obsolete as changes in customer bases, competition and the rate of change itself alter the marketplace. Post-industrial companies must be "reengineered," which necessitates starting anew, going back to the beginning to invent a better way of accomplishing tasks. The process requires a leader with vision using information technologies, consulting closely with suppliers to reduce inventories, and empowering employees so that decision-making becomes part of the work.

In this book, a departure from the traditional orientation of companies on the basis of division of labor and a reorientation toward business process reengineering (BPR) had thus been propagated, which triggered an extensive wave of activities in this direction. Note that not just a *modeling* of (business) processes had been demanded, but rather their immediate *reengineering*, therefore its complete revision and realignment. Business process modeling and management subsequently became a central subject in many enterprises, where appropriate models and tools were required. For the description of business processes, *process models* are used, which generally employ a graphical notation and which try to establish a common "language" between managers, business leaders, and decision makers as well as for departments.

As already mentioned, Petri nets are used in this book to model business processes. The reasons are numerous and are explained elsewhere. The foundations for Petri nets were already laid in 1962 by Carl Adam Petri in his dissertation *Communication with Machines* (which was written in German). On the one hand, Petri nets have been frequently examined; on the other hand, they have become an important, precise tool in the description of processes. The reasons for this lie in the principally simple applicability of Petri nets and in tool support, as offered by the *Horus* system, for example.

The literature on Petri nets is very extensive and describes many different classes of networks, which have been suggested and studied over the years. For use in Horus, we focus on just one specific network class, which appears particularly appropriate for the modeling objectives pursued here—the *XML nets*. These will be introduced later in this chapter; for a better prior understanding in simple form, we introduce the basics of Petri nets first.

The most important terms that are used in this context are:

- Business processes
- Objects
- Organization structure
- Roles and resources

Business processes (hereafter simply *processes*) describe business-relevant procedures in an enterprise, an establishment, an administration, or public authority, and basically disassemble an entire task occurring in the frame of a commercial activity, as appropriately as possible into partial processes, and these again into subtasks or *activities*. The activities constituting a process or partial process are connected by exchangeable information, data, objects, or also documents, which are often created by an activity and read by a subsequent activity, altered, or also removed (deleted). Processes are particularly structured hierarchically, that is, built up from subprocesses, when they are complex, therefore containing many case differentiations or many activities and complex relationships within these, or if parts are to be reused as subprocesses.

Processes and the activities therein are executed by *resources*, which may be human resources (employees of the business in question or external business partners) or machine resources (computers, programs, or services). Activities of executable employees generally originate from the *organization structure* of the enterprise in question, within which they can often assume different *roles* (e.g., by a predefined representation regulation in the case of illness or vacation).

As a simple example to illustrate these concepts, let us look at an inventory procedure shown in Fig. 3.1, where items that are no longer sold are removed from the enterprise inventory. The entire process consists of the activities Check assortment, Remove item from assortment, and Inform procurement: discontinued item. As part of the annual inventory, an examination of the complete product assortment is conducted, which product management carries out as organization unit in charge. The trigger for this activity sets forth a demand for inventory. After the examination, a tested product assortment exists; articles which are no longer sold are removed by product management assistance; as a result of this activity, a list of items to be deleted from the product assortment is available. The enterprise procurement will now be informed by product management of the articles that are no longer to be procured.

We therefore consider processes as a combination or composition of activities, where it is obvious that not all processes run in a purely sequential manner. We will see later that processes may also include branching, parallel parts or cyclic repetitions (cycles); composite or nested process structures (the above-mentioned subprocesses) are also conceivable. Frequently, single or multiple activities are executed simultaneously or iterated in the context of loops or cyclic repetitions. Synchronizations are occasionally needed at the end of parallel subprocesses, to

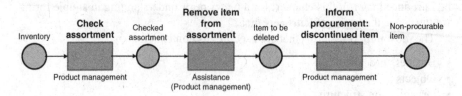

Fig. 3.1 Possible procedure of an inventory

ensure that, for example, the subprocesses are both completed before any further activities can be started.

The procedure described above in Fig. 3.1 already includes references to particular employees from parts of the enterprise, which will be responsible for the implementation of each activity; here, this is still roughly applied to units such as `Product management` or `Assistance (Product management)`. In other contexts, this may be broken down to the individual person, for example, if it is important that only certain employees who hold a relevant training will or should be allowed to execute certain activities. The sequence of operations also contains information about the objects, which are present between the individual activities at the beginning as well as at the end of the process.

It can be seen from this small example already—and again we look back to the situation with Confusio AG described in Chap. 1—that modeling of such processes is of central importance for understanding the procedures in an enterprise. Such modeling is carried out in accordance with the segmentation above for the following areas (see Fig. 3.2):

- Process (procedure) modeling
- Object modeling
- Organization modeling

During *process modeling*, all processes of an enterprise or of the respective application area are recorded. These can be different types of processes, such as business-critical, administrative, or supporting processes. With process modeling, a procedure that fixes a guideline for the single modeler is essential, with which the modeling can be performed. One may proceed, for example, from bottom to top ("bottom-up"), initially modeling individual activities, then gradually combining these into larger units (subprocesses and processes). One can also, and this will be our approach, proceed from top to bottom ("top-down"), first providing an initial overview of the highest level of abstraction at which the core business processes of the company are identified; these are then gradually refined. As we shall see, it is important in general for the procedure to focus first on the regular execution of the processes ("nice-weather flight"), then to gradually include possible exceptions or error cases. A method for process modeling which has proven itself in numerous practice cases is the *Horus method*; this will be presented in Chap. 4.

The objects and/or documents required by activities and processes are modeled in *object modeling*. Here, it is conceivable that a class diagram is created that describes, for example, in the notation of the Unified Modeling Language (UML) which object schemes or classes of a particular scope underlie which attributes and methods. However, it is also conceivable—and this shall happen here in the course of our further development—that one describes the object and document structures in XML notation, which shall be exchanged between activities and subprocesses. The benefits of using XML will be addressed later; however, we will use a graphical notation for the sake of clarity, as it was already used in Fig. 2.3 in the form of the object model as well as in Fig. 2.4.

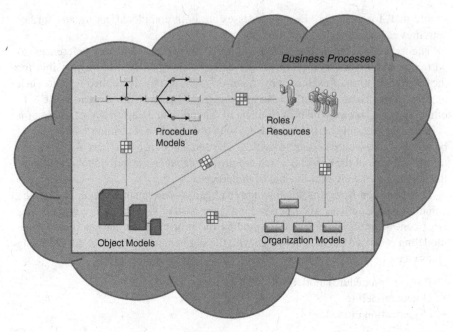

Fig. 3.2 Key aspects of business process modeling

Finally, in *organization modeling*, the essential parts of the underlying organi-zation are depicted, usually in the form of a hierarchy that includes the executive board as the highest level, followed by departments or areas such as purchasing, warehousing, product management, or sales. This was demonstrated exemplarily in Fig. 2.5. The number of layers used depends on the structure of the enterprise, or the desired or required level of detail in the modeling.

In the following, we will see that it is advisable to consider the three aspects of process, object, and organization modeling as a whole and to pursue them concurrently, since the situation found in an enterprise most of the time corresponds to the situation shown in Fig. 3.3: The organization structure of an enterprise in no way limits the processes running in the enterprise; processes instead connect different parts of the organization in various ways.

Here, we mention only some of the aspects which can be taken into account by a common modeling of processes, objects, and organization units: Top-down process modeling allows to stipulate objectives and strategies for the entire project at the outset of a modeling project. A typical goal (both from modeling in particular as well as business process management in general, see Fig. 2.6) is the streamlining of processes, the elimination of redundancies, increasing efficiency and, the creation of transparency. For this, powerful organization structures are necessary so that processes can be handled efficiently, and at the same time, can adjust to continuously changing requirements. Furthermore, process transparency serves as a risk assessment as well as an improvement in communications of the

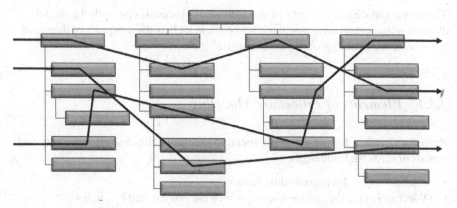

Fig. 3.3 Organization structure vs. process procedures

participating departments of the various processes involved. To measure whether the desired objectives are achieved, the definition of *performance indicators* is required, against which success can be measured. At the level of individual employees or individual departments, a knowledge map, or a so-called *skill map*, often arises as a by-product of the process modeling, which will ascertain the competencies for individuals, which they must possess or have acquired in the context of specific processes. These aspects will be discussed in detail in Chap. 4.

In the following section, we describe the various modeling constructs necessary for the modeling activities just described.

3.3 Modeling Constructs for Business Processes

In the modeling of business processes, the individual processes and their rules are gathered and illustrated with graphic models. With the help of these models (and other models such as context models, key figures, business rules, objective, or risk models, see Chap. 4), the individual processes as well as all involved resources, the processed objects, and all other relevant details can be illustrated. The knowledge associated with this information can be used, on the one hand, for the review and improvement of business processes. On the other hand, business process modeling is an effective way to summarize information adequately and to make this information available to all parties involved.

Procedure modeling is at the central point of business process modeling. It offers the possibility of depicting the individual business operations in so-called *procedure nets*. Using these procedure nets, also called *procedure models*, procedures from all areas of an enterprise can be portrayed. The modeler generally starts with a rough representation of the complete business process; in subsequent steps, single sections are refined and the different procedure models are then connected with one other.

The scope and degree of detail of the individual processes rest with the modeler's discretion; important are a structured approach as well as the adequacy of the results in terms of the overall goals of the enterprise.

3.3.1 Elements of Procedure Modeling

Procedure models have a simple, structured design in the case of Petri nets and consist of three basic elements:

- *Activities* that are represented by rectangles
- *Object stores* (in the broadest sense) which are represented by circles
- *Connections* between activities and object stores that are represented by directed edges

Procedure models show which activities are carried out when and under what conditions in a business process; as a first example, the reader should compare the explanations given above for Fig. 3.1.

In procedure models, *activities* are represented as rectangles. They process the objects located in the single object stores. Activities can consume, create, or read objects. At the same time, one distinguishes different procedure types that are clarified in another place. Activities can be provided with attributes (properties), such as the cost of the activity, its duration, and the intervals of its execution. Later this will be explained in detail. What is important for creating readable models is that activities can be characterized as operations by using *verbs* during name selection. This supports the clarity of the model and is essential if one wants to replace individual elements in created models, for design reasons, with graphics or pictures.

Object stores are represented as circles in procedure models. They include objects, where the name of the object store should clearly state which items are stored there. Through this, the comprehensibility of a model is improved. Object stores may also be assigned a certain capacity. The capacity specifies the maximum number of objects that can be simultaneously located within the object store. It is specified hereafter by "$C = \ldots$" in the model. It should also be noted that one can define further attributes for an object store, such as cost or storage period. These attributes influence the execution of the activities. This will be explained in the further course of our discussion.

To model a specific procedure, activities and object stores are linked. There are several types of connections, which are symbolized by different kinds of arrows:

- *Input connections* (see Fig. 3.4): The activity consumes objects from the input object store during execution.
- *Output connections* (see Fig. 3.5): The activity creates objects during execution and stores these in the output object store.

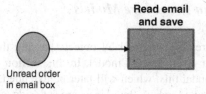

Fig. 3.4 Input connection

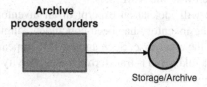

Fig. 3.5 Output connection

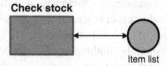

Fig. 3.6 Update connection

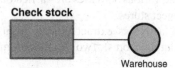

Fig. 3.7 Read connection

- *Update connections* (see Fig. 3.6): The activity modifies objects in the related object store during execution.
- *Read connections* (see Fig. 3.7): The activity accesses the objects in a read-only manner during execution; the objects are neither changed nor removed from the object store.

One also can define attributes for pairs of connections and object stores, for example, the probability with which the connection is executed (e.g., after a branching). Another attribute can be the number of objects that are consumed or created by the connection.

The description of the basic elements of procedure modeling used here, and in the following, is now complete. With these, different processes can be represented statically. To be able to capture the *dynamics* of a process, the "state" of this process must be modeled at different times. It will be shown where the objects are located at different times or which object is being processed at a given time by which activity and how. We will consider this next.

3.3.2 Dynamics in Procedure Models

Dynamics in procedures is expressed by objects passing through the individual steps or activities of a given process model. In this section, we will first look at the simplest way to model this, which will later be extended. To this end, a dot, a so-called *token*, is specified, where the objects are set aside at a particular time. As will be seen, this approach may be illustrative, but it is not very efficient yet; so we will further extend it below to the XML nets.

As an example, we will look at an excerpt of an inventory process shown in Fig. 3.1 above. After the inventory has been concluded, single items are removed from the assortment of the enterprise. Such an item will appear in the input store of the relevant activity as a token and is transferred by the activity into the output store. This is illustrated in Figs. 3.8 and 3.9.

In a sequential procedure, dynamics are relatively simple; however, capacities for the single object stores may already be significant (e.g., how many parts of a certain type can be in the warehouse). Obviously, it will become more complex when branches, loops, and other process structures are used in a procedure model. We will discuss the dynamics of such structures next.

Basically, in procedure models, nothing more happens than that the objects "wander" from one activity to the next. The models thus show the possible "paths" that the objects may take. At what time the objects "wander" from one activity to the next or at which time the various activities are carried out depends, therefore, on the state of the adjacent object stores.

As already mentioned, activities extract objects from their input stores and deposit objects in their output stores. Two conditions must be met for this to happen:

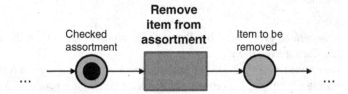

Fig. 3.8 Item before being removed from assortment

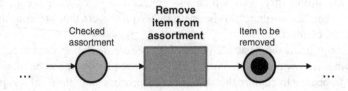

Fig. 3.9 Item after being removed from assortment

1. The necessary number of objects must be available in all input stores of the activity.
2. In all output stores of the activity, the required number of objects can be deposited.

If these conditions are met, the activity can be executed (it can "fire"). It then takes the required number of objects from each input store and deposits the appropriate number of objects in each output store.

This is obvious with sequential processes such as the last shown example. However, what happens when the process is no longer strictly sequential? In such cases, the exact number of tokens considered is essential. Firstly, we will examine the case of simple branching: A confirmation e-mail as well as an order object shall be generated after submitting an online order. The situation shown in Fig. 3.10 exists prior to the execution of this activity. With the execution of the activity, each of the two output stores will be supplied with a token, as shown in Fig. 3.11.

If one has defined a capacity for the respective object store, the number of objects is then represented by tokens which are present in the object store at that particular time; this is shown in Fig. 3.12 for a capacity of $C = 10$. In this case, through the execution of the activity Submit order as in the previous example, a token from the input store has been removed; both output stores are allocated with one token

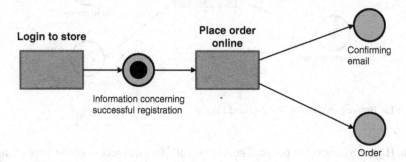

Fig. 3.10 Object store before placing the online order

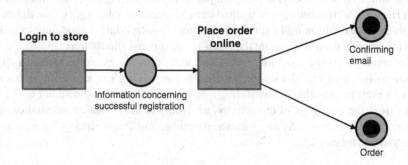

Fig. 3.11 Object store after placing the online order

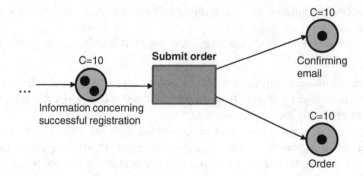

Fig. 3.12 Object store with capacities

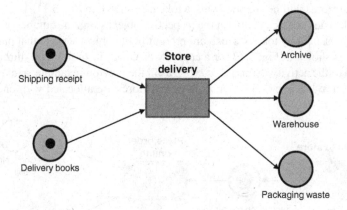

Fig. 3.13 Before execution of Store delivery

each. Higher numbers are possible here, as for all shown object stores an upper limit capacity of 10 has been established.

It should already be pointed out here that a modeler does not have to represent the conditions of the models at different points in time during procedure modeling with Horus. This is taken care of by the Horus Simulation components. One defines the so-called execution times for the individual activities during modeling, which the Horus Simulation component then uses for its process simulations.

Dynamic procedure modeling is clarified with a further example. Consider the situation shown in Fig. 3.13, which states that a packing list as well as a book delivery must be available before storing a delivery. The situation shown in Fig. 3.14 arises from the execution of the activity; according to the transition rule indicated above, the output stores Archive, Warehouse, and Packaging waste are allocated one token each.

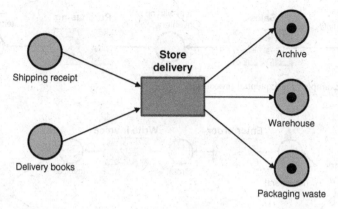

Fig. 3.14 After execution of `Store delivery`

3.3.3 Procedure Types

In two small examples, we have seen thus far that procedures in processes do not always proceed in a strictly sequential manner. In practice, it will even be the norm that procedures branch and are then executed simultaneously, or in parts, in parallel, which is often desirable to increase the execution efficiency. Furthermore, it will occur that parallel or concurrent procedures again converge at a specific point so that, for example, a comparison can be made to determine whether the subprocedures can be completed within a specified time frame. Often, there are parts in complex processes that run independently, and then, there is the case of single or multiple branching of procedures, for example, to allow certain special cases, special conditions, exceptions, or possible error situations to be taken into consideration.

The following figures show these types of situations:

- Figure 3.15 shows an example of a sequential procedure (similar to the one that was already shown earlier in Fig. 3.1): The activities successively follow a fixed order.
- Figure 3.16 shows an example of concurrent[1] activities: The individual activities run parallel in parts in this case. In this phase, they are not chronologically dependent on one another.
- Figure 3.17 shows an example of alternative procedures: Several process sequences are possible here. Only one of these is actually executed within a process instance, however.

---

[1]Occasionally, "concurrently" is used here as a synonym of "in parallel," although strictly speaking the two notions differ.

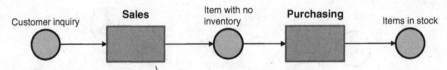

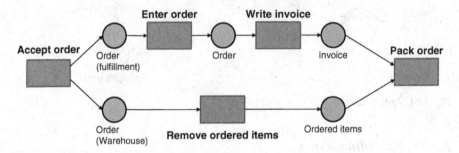

Fig. 3.15 Example of a sequential procedure

Fig. 3.16 Example of concurrent activities

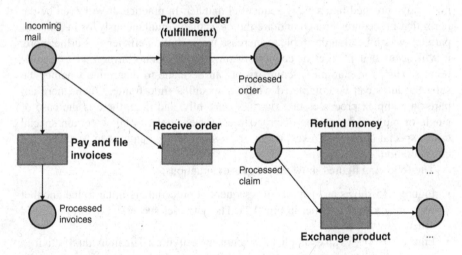

Fig. 3.17 Example of alternative procedures

In alternative procedures that are made possible by branching in the procedure model, several possibilities exist to handle the objects. Here, the aforementioned attributes of activities, object stores, and connections, or the resulting rules for the procedure sequence, decide which activity is performed and when.

If procedures branch, which is the case in the modeling of parallel sections or alternatives, the individual procedures can then by all means end separately. In most cases, however, they are conflated again at a later time. In such a case, one

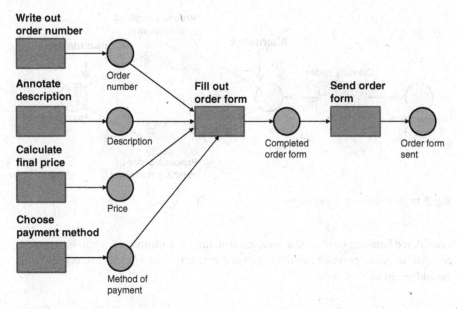

Fig. 3.18 Example of a synchronization

speaks of either *synchronization* or *consolidation*. Sometimes it is necessary that multiple objects are available for the execution of an activity. This is made clear by merging the respective object stores as input store of the activity in question. The so far independent activity results are synchronized at this point. An example of a synchronization is shown in Fig. 3.18; all presumed activities must be completed to execute the activity Fill out order form. In addition to synchronization, consolidation also exists. Several activities are consolidated again according to an alternative (also alternative procedure). An example of a consolidation is shown in Fig. 3.19; one of the alternatively possible activities is executed here, after which the process continues sequentially.

For a better understanding of synchronization, we refer the reader to Exercise 3.2 at the end of this chapter which deals with traffic lights.

The Petri nets considered up to now were invariably "flat" in the sense that activities and object stores were always at the same level of abstraction. In addition, the tokens used in object stores until now had no attributes or inner structure. Evidently, both aspects are not sufficient for the modeling of real-world business processes (see also Sect. 3.3.5): Business processes, on one hand, are often complex so that one subdivides them into hierarchically arranged subprocesses for better readability; formally, this is achieved by a *refinement* of a given Petri net, which we will discuss in the next subsection. On the other hand, the objects which are moved and considered in the context of business processes are not single bits (i.e., simple tokens) but invoices, orders, or other documents that themselves, like processes, must be modeled appropriately. We recall from Chap. 2 (see Fig. 2.3) that the objects

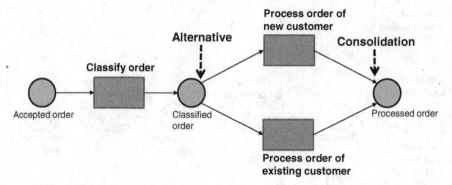

Fig. 3.19 Example of a consolidation

considered here can bear quite a complex structure and, ultimately, are to be mapped to XML documents which are then used in XML nets. The modeling of objects will be addressed in Sect. 3.4.

3.3.4 Refinement

We continue next to what we have already addressed in Chap. 2, in connection with Figs. 2.1 and 2.2: The refinement of activities (see Sect. 2.2). As already mentioned, the modeler decides how detailed the various processes are to be modeled. The degree of detail of a process model can depend on, for example, how many exemptions from regular procedures or how many possible error cases will or need to be taken into account. However, if too many elements are arranged in a model, it becomes complex, difficult to read, and difficult to understand. As shown in Chap. 4, while presenting the Horus Modeling Method, one usually begins, therefore, with an abstract and rough representation of all process structures, which are included in the so-called *business process architecture model* of an enterprise. This represents the highest hierarchical level for the phased modeling of business processes and relevant information. It defines the key processes that are considered in the framework of the modeling project. The business processes at this level of abstraction are referred to as *core business processes*. Based on the modeled overview contained within the project definition, business processes are modeled top-down hierarchically at different levels of abstraction. Generally, no objects are yet specified at the top-level of the core business processes.

With this approach, which is widely used in practice, individual activities are then refined until the desired level of detail is achieved. The required information can then be displayed in a clear and structured form, yet remaining flexible. Furthermore, changes are possible at the different refinement levels without other levels being affected.

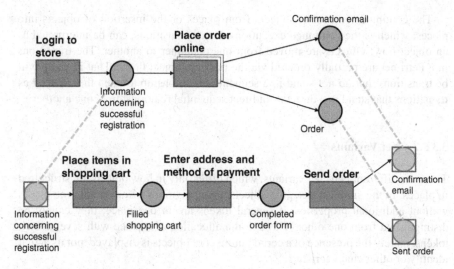

Fig. 3.20 Example of a refinement

To ensure a structurally correct design, care must be taken that an activity to be refined matches the adjoining object store as well as the entry and exit points of the refinement. If one creates a refinement of an activity in Horus, the tool then automatically prepares a copy of every object store connected to the activity in the refinement diagram. The copies created are graphically characterized by a rectangle around the object store representation. This is shown in Fig. 3.20 for activity `Place order online`.

3.3.5 Object Stores in Petri Nets: XML Nets

3.3.5.1 Process Description with Petri Nets

Petri nets describe processes that consist of activities on objects. Activities represent state transitions from an initial state to a successor state; in Petri nets, these are called *transitions*. Objects are stored in containers and can be an input or output object of an activity. The object containers are called *places*. A process state is defined by the assignment of objects to all places. Places can be empty, that is, not occupied by an object.

A transition can take place (or *fire*) in a given process state if the necessary objects exist in the input places and, at the same time, the objects to be created do not yet exist in the output places. A transition is then *activated* or *enabled*. If an enabled transition takes place (fires), objects are removed from the input places and are added to the output places.

The continual removal of objects from places or the insertion of objects into places, which is the continued execution of state transitions, can be interpreted as an object flow: Objects are moved from one container to another. The transitions in a Petri net are partially ordered via the possible object flows. That is, there will be transitions that do not stand in a sequential relationship to one other as well as transitions that stand in a direct or indirect sequential relationship to one another.

3.3.5.2 Net Variants

There are different Petri net variants, which differ only in how objects are structured in places. In the simplest case, the objects are anonymous tokens within the places without additional properties. If several tokens are in one place, they cannot be distinguished from one other. Through the allocation of a place with several such tokens, merely the presence of a certain number of objects is displayed, not its actual identity or other characteristics.

The places (as they represent containers) can be assigned individual capacity values which determine the maximum number of objects located within the place in question. If no capacity value is explicitly specified, an unlimited place capacity is then assumed. If the capacity of a place is equal to 1, then the number of objects in an arbitrary process condition can only be 0 or 1 within this place. This place can therefore be interpreted as a *condition* that is fulfilled (truth value is 1) if a token is present and is not fulfilled (truth value 0) otherwise.

Objects contained within a place can also have individual qualities in so-called *higher* Petri nets. In particular, they are distinctly identifiable via a key. In *Predicate/Transition nets* (Pr/T nets), places are interpreted as relation types, and tokens are tuples of the corresponding relation. Thus, a Pr/T net represents processes involving the data of a relational database. Activities in Pr/T nets remove or insert tuples into relations.

In a Petri net, edges can be labeled with so-called *filters*. In the simplest case, this is an integer stating how many objects are removed from the adjacent input place when firing a transition or how many objects are to be inserted into the corresponding output place when firing a transition. As a "default," the designation of all edges in a Petri net equals 1, that is, one token is inserted or removed if that transition fires.

In higher Petri nets, edges can be marked with *constants*, which stipulate that only objects with corresponding values can be inserted or removed over that edge. In addition, edges can be labeled with variables that can be allocated with diverse constant values. In Pr/T nets, tuples consisting of variables and constants are added to the edges as a label, which—similar to the database language Query-By-Example—exemplarily indicate which tuples are removed or inserted from the respective place.

In principle, the structure of permissible objects in the places of a higher Petri net can be specified with an arbitrary data model. This is Codd's relational model in Pr/T nets. There are several proposals in which object models are used for typing places. Tokens then represent complexly structured objects (i.e., the objects can again be composed of other objects). Filters as an edge inscription must be defined according to the data model used; query languages of the respective data model normally present themselves for this.

3.3.5.3 XML Nets

In *XML nets*, a special variant of higher Petri nets, the objects in the places are XML documents. XML documents are hierarchically structured and consist of XML elements that can again be composed of XML documents.

The places in an XML net are containers for XML documents. The structure for a permissible place ("valid") XML document can be defined using a DTD (*Document Type Definition*), that is, a formal (context-free) grammar (with regular expressions on the right-hand sides of production rules), or using XML Schema. Permitted objects in a place must fulfill the corresponding DTD or correspond to the respective XML Schema specification.

An XML net describes a class of processes on XML objects. A single sequence in the Petri net represents a specific process instance. In Pr/T nets, objects (tuples) are indivisible: They are removed from or inserted into places during firing as a whole, the parallel execution of multiple activities on such a tuple is therefore not possible (as only one activity may access the tuple at a given time). In XML nets, the objects in places are (possibly) hierarchically structured XML documents. Transitions can therefore also access a partial document, that is, remove parts from objects in input places and insert new parts into existing objects in output places. In particular, it is also possible to model the parallel execution of multiple activities in different parts of the same object, such as when two authors process different chapters of the same document.

The filters that are added to edges in XML nets are hierarchically structured— corresponding to the structure of XML documents in the incident place. There are various options for description languages for these filters, such as the XML path description language XPath or the XML query language XQuery. As with other higher Petri net variants, the additional possibility exists in XML nets to use logical expressions as transition inscriptions, which are formulated over the variable in the edge inscriptions of the edges incident to the transition, to establish rules to describe the removal of objects from places or the insertion of objects into places.

The activation state of a transition in an XML net is generally defined in exactly the same way as in other Petri net variants. A transition is activated for a given process state (i.e., a given allocation of the places with XML documents) if certain XML documents exist in the input places of these transitions and if certain XML documents do not exist in the output places of the transitions. The XML elements to be removed or inserted can be specified with the edge inscriptions and the transition inscription.

When a transition fires in a XML net, objects are removed from the input places according to the incidental edge inscription of the respective place and under consideration of the transition inscription, and objects are annexed concurrently into the output places under consideration of the incidental edge inscription of the respective output place. Insertion can mean that an XML element is inserted into an existing XML document or that a new XML document is stored in the place. Appropriately, removal can mean that an XML element is removed from an available XML document or that a complete XML document is removed from the place. The distinction between both insert and remove variations is made by corresponding labeling of the respective filter at the edge in question.

To increase transparency and to simplify modeling, we use several abbreviations for the edges: Undirected edges between two nodes k_1 and k_2 are shortened versions for two arrows, respectively, one of which is directed from k_1 to k_2 and the other from k_2 to k_1, whereby both edges are equally labeled. Access to a place, which is connected to a transition over an undirected edge, is "reading," that is, the allocation of the corresponding place is not altered by firing the transition (see Fig. 3.7). Occasionally, in practice, "edge branching" is also used as an abbreviated form for several edges that have either a common output node, or a common destination node (or both); it should be noted that this may lead to confusion.

3.4 Object Modeling

3.4.1 Requirements

For comprehensive management of business processes, the definition of the business object structures to be processed is necessary, in addition to the definition of the procedures; this will be addressed in this section. For modeling of business object structures when used with XML nets, the following requirements arise:

1. The structures of the business objects must be definable with attributes and relations.
2. The representation should be clear and understandable for the business departments and should deliver a formally exact presentation of facts for the IT department, so that it can be also used for software generators.
3. Modeling of business object structures must be possible, independent of the respective business process, to allow for modeling business object structures for a project, a business area, or the complete enterprise.
4. On the other hand, single components of the business object structures must be in a position to be fixed or summarized to objects which are processed in a certain step of a business process. For example, at the approval step of an order, only the header of the order bearing the total amount is required and not the individual order lines. When creating the order, however, the complete order header and the individual order items are required. The modeling of the business object structures must therefore include the definition of simple structures in the form of individual components, such as the order header and order line, which then

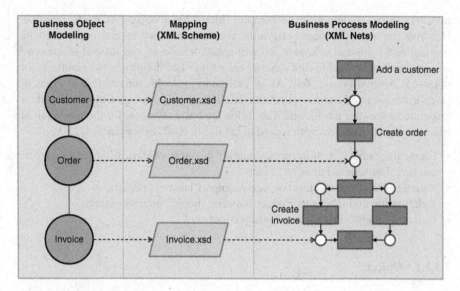

Fig. 3.21 Allocation of business object structures to business processes

can be linked to corresponding relations. Furthermore, the aggregation of simple business object structures, such as Order header and Order line, into a complex business object structure Order must also be possible.

5. Corresponding XML Schema documents must be generated and assigned to the XML nets based on the modeled business object structures. Figure 3.21 shows the modeling of business object structures, business processes, and the allocation of business object structures to business processes on the basis of XML Schema and XML nets.

In complex projects, processes and structures can initially be processed separately and subsequently be brought together with a business object structure/business process mapping in further steps. Alternatively, business process and business object structure definitions may also emanate together, if by the project structure, that is, based on the knowledge and the division of labor of a team, it is possible or even necessary.

3.4.2 Notation Used

As notation for object modeling, a combination of specific concepts from *Asset-Oriented Modeling* (AOM), UML class diagrams, and *Entity-Relationship* (ER) or the *Extended Entity-Relationship* (EER) model is used which favorably fulfills the requirements. The basis of the model used here is AOM, as this method basically comes closer to the goal of the modeling of business object structures for XML networks, since a definition of complex hierarchical objects is made possible. However, certain differences exist in the notation described here as opposed to the original AOM. Instead of *assets*, we will speak of *objects*, and instead of *arcs*, we will speak of *relationship and inheritance edges*. The definition of operations for objects is omitted here in full. As an extension to AOM, three different types of so-called *collective conditions* to define consistency rules between objects and their associated edges are introduced. The following basic elements for the modeling of business object structures with regard to the use in XML nets exist:

- Elementary object with attributes (simple business object). Elementary objects are hereafter referred to as an object.
- Aggregation of (elementary) objects (complex business object).
- Relationship and inheritance edges between simple business objects.
- Collective constraints for relationship edges.

3.4.2.1 Object

An *object* is a container to combine the attributes of business objects into logical units. It has a unique name, optionally one or more keys, attributes with appropriate data types and, if necessary, constraints. Objects are represented as rectangles with rounded corners. Copy objects can be used to make the representation of complex models easier to understand. They have the same semantics as their original objects yet can be tied to arbitrary many positions of a diagram. Copy objects are represented by a dotted line, the contents of which cannot be changed. Figure 3.22 shows the representation of an object and a copy object.

3.4.2.2 Relationship and Inheritance Edges Between Objects

Edges between objects are elements which depict relationships and dependencies between the objects. There are two types of edges:

A *relationship edge* represents a relation between objects according to the semantics of the ER model. Two descriptions can be stored with relationship edges, one description per edge end among the connected objects. The descriptions refer to the outbound direction starting from the respective object. Theoretically, three basic types of relationship edges between objects are available: $1 : 1$, $1 : n$, and

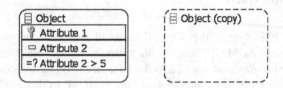

Fig. 3.22 Object and object copy

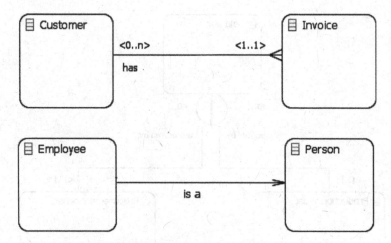

Fig. 3.23 Relationship edge and inheritance edge

$n : m$, which are represented in the "crow's feet" notation. Furthermore, the detail cardinalities must be indicated for each end of an edge.

An *inheritance edge* represents an inheritance between objects. An inheritance edge bears the description "is a." Inheritance is represented by a simple arrow. The direction of the arrow signifies an inheritance edge, representing that the output object is a specialization of the target object. Against the direction of the arrow means that the output object is a generalization of the target object.

Figure 3.23 shows a $1 : n$ relationship edge between Customer and Invoice, which is labeled with cardinalities at both ends, that is, a customer can have multiple invoices, but is also permitted not to have an invoice. As a second example, an inheritance edge is represented between Employee and Person. It describes that an employee is a person, that is, all attributes of Person are passed on to Employee.

3.4.2.3 Collective Constraints for Connections Between Objects

Additional collective constraints can be defined for relationship edges. Collective constraints are positioned between objects and relational edges and are represented by a corresponding icon attached to the object. There are three types of collective constraints, which appropriately expand the semantics of the objects and relationship edges that have been introduced up to this point:

An *XOR collective constraint* is an *exclusive OR* of the relationship edges attached to the collective condition, that is, for an instance of the object exactly one relationship instance of the affiliated XOR relationship edges may exist.

An *OR collective constraint* is an *OR with at least one selection*. In an OR collective constraint, at least one relationship instance must be available. Several relationship instances can also exist, however.

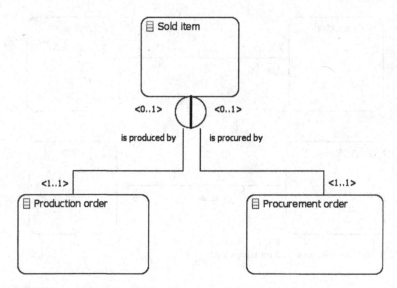

Fig. 3.24 XOR collective constraint

A *SIM collective constraint* is a *simultaneity*. A SIM collective constraint must be present in the existence of a relationship instance connected at the collecting constraint and also simultaneously available for all relationship instances corresponding to other connected edges.

Figure 3.24 shows an example of an XOR collective constraint. It is expressed in the represented example that a sold product is either manufactured by a production order or purchased with a procurement contract.

Figure 3.25 shows an example of an OR collective constraint. The illustrated example shows that an order may contain any number of services or any number of items. An order, however, must include at least one service or one item as an alternative.

Figure 3.26 shows an example of a SIM collective constraint. The illustrated example shows that if a sales order is created for a customer-specific, that is, individually manufactured product, a corresponding internal production order must be created.

Certain circumstances can or must be modeled without collective constraints. In Fig. 3.27, the first example shows a flexible or-connection which, in contrast to the model shown in Fig. 3.24, allows that for a sold product neither a production nor a purchase order need be generated, as a product can also be in stock. On the other hand, a production and a purchase order each could be generated for a sold product. The second example shows that with an ordered item, a product and a working employee must be allocated. These connection instances are both mandatory but have no dependencies between themselves and refer only to the corresponding object, in contrast to the SIM collective constraint in Fig. 3.26.

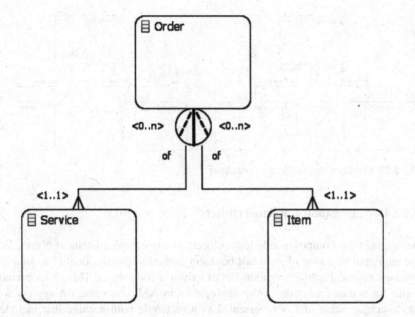

Fig. 3.25 OR collective constraint

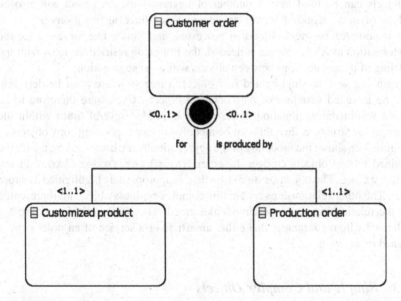

Fig. 3.26 SIM collective constraint

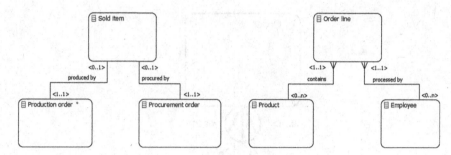

Fig. 3.27   Objects without collective constraints

3.4.2.4   Aggregation of Related Objects

An aggregation composes individual objects into a complex business object. For the aggregation, a root object must be distinguished to clearly identify a complex business object. Each aggregation has exactly one root object. This is the prerequisite for a transformation of the aggregation in XML Schema. An aggregation has a unique name and is represented as a rectangle with a name that includes the corresponding objects, together with the root object. The root object of the aggregation is marked by a highlighted (bold) border.

Objects can be used in any number of aggregations. An object can also be used as often as required within an aggregation. Since aggregations are to be used as complex business objects in processes, and thus a tree structure for the transformation to XML schema is needed, the following restrictions exist with the modeling of the connections between objects within an aggregation:

Beginning with the highlighted root object, a tree structure must be derivable from the modeled structure of the contained objects. Cycles are therefore to be avoided within the aggregation. If an object is needed several times within the context of the structure, then this can be modeled by corresponding copy objects.

Figure 3.28 shows the modeling of the aggregation `Purchase order` with the contained related objects `Order header`, `Supplier`, `Order line`, `Item`, and `Services`. The object `Order header` is appropriately highlighted as a root object. The other relationships within this complex business object are represented with the relationship edges previously described. The XOR collective constraint for the order item guarantees that either an article or a service of an order item is assigned in any case.

3.4.3   Simple and Complex Objects

Based on the concepts described, business objects can be defined as follows: A *business object* is a data structure that is defined with the elements *object*, *edge*, *aggregation*, and *collective constraint*. There is a distinction between simple and complex business objects:

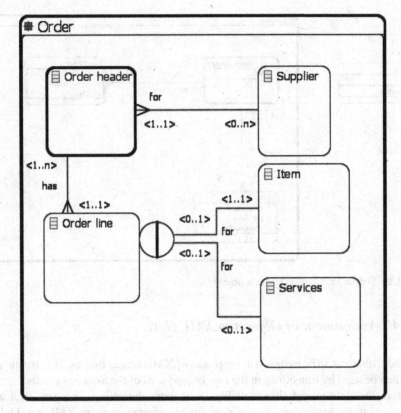

Fig. 3.28 Aggregation of related objects

1. Objects provide *simple* business objects. A simple business object includes all attributes with data types, keys, and simple constraints of the corresponding object. Edges to other objects, collective constraints, and the affinity to aggregations are not considered in simple business objects.
2. Aggregations provide *complex* business objects. A complex business object contains all information according to (1) of the simple business objects contained, the edges within the aggregation and their collective constraints.

Figure 3.29 shows the difference between simple and complex business objects. Aggregation Customer describes a complex business object, since it possesses several interrelated relationships of objects. Object Customer is marked as the root object and delivers its own keys as well as the keys of the complex business object. Object Item, however, is a simple business object, since it contains no other objects. The relationship between the business objects takes place at the level of the objects. Thus, items and customer could be connected via a relationship edge between the objects Item and Customer account.

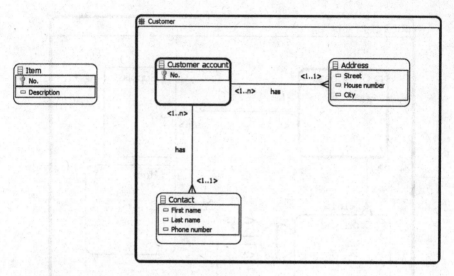

Fig. 3.29 Simple and complex business objects

3.4.4   Assignment of Objects to XML Nets

Business objects can be assigned to the places of XML nets as tokens. The structures can then be used by transitions in the pre- or post-area of the assigned places.

From the data model shown in Fig. 3.29, both the object Item as well as the aggregation Customer can be used for an assignment to an XML net. Only the simple business object Customer account of the complex business object could be used for an assignment, for example.

3.5   Organization Modeling

For the final area, we turn to organization modeling. We have already noted in various places that process activities can be assigned to persons who execute these. For this, one refers back to the organization to which these persons belong, and to this end, it is reasonable to first describe this organization in a model as well. The goal is to depict relevant organizational units and their relationships in a given company or the relevant business units among one another. In this respect, recall Fig. 3.3 which shows that organization structure and process modeling are, in a sense, "orthogonal" to one another.

In organization modeling, the individual organization units are depicted as rectangles. In these rectangles, different types of information for each organization unit are displayed (see the organization structure of the distribution area in Fig. 2.5). The hierarchical relationships of the organization units will be represented as connections.

When designing a new organization structure, two aspects should be considered: the division of labor and its coordination. The *division of labor* is the subdivision of the single organization units according to areas of responsibility. The possibility exists to carry out the segmentation by the various activities within the process flow (such as purchase, production, sales, administration, etc.). This is called "functional organization." Alternatively, one can divide the units by factors such as products, regions or customers. The organization is then "object related." It should be noted that object related organizations are often called "process related." The formed units in this case are responsible for the execution of a task from beginning to end (e.g., execution of a project). Depending on the scope, the division is carried out up to the individual positions (smallest organization unit).

We also mention that in such hierarchical models, a "complete" or an "incomplete" decomposition is possible. In the first case, the primary (superordinate) box is a clip for the secondary (subordinate), having no other function than to lead the secondary. In the second case of an incomplete decomposition, it will be brought forth that the primary box can also have its own functions (and not only the function of leading and coordination of the secondary).

In order for the business process to take place as smoothly as possible, the individual process flows (and the persons involved) must be compatible or coordinated with one another, respectively. For this purpose, "task bundles" are created. It is no longer necessary that all individual positions have to be coordinated, since now the different areas (according to the bundling) can be addressed. The coordination effort is hence reduced.

When classifying and also when representing organization units, different types can be distinguished:

- Internal organization units, including staff positions (this refers to organization units that advise in special subjects or are responsible for all questions addressed to the primary unit)
- External organization units

We will not further distinguish this graphically at this point.

As with process modeling, the opportunity also exists in organization modeling to *refine* the individual organization units. In a refinement, an organizational unit can be broken down into smaller units and thus be represented in greater detail. External organization units form an exception here. They are usually not detailed further (e.g., an organization unit Customer). Analogous to the procedure in the process modeling, it should also be ensured that the level of abstraction within one model remains constant. As an example, in Fig. 2.5, the organization unit Sales Management has been refined into the organizational units Sales Support, Sales Germany, EMEA Sales, and Sales RoW.[2]

The main goal of organization modeling is to identify and assign resources for the execution of process instances. By *resources*, persons or objects of an organization

---

[2]EMEA stands for *Europe, Middle East, Africa*; RoW stands for *rest of the world*.

are meant which are responsible for the execution of activities. Resources perceive so-called *roles* and are assigned to specific organizational units. They are therefore documented in connection with "their" organization units. Since the functional fields and qualifications of a resource are often different, resources sometimes assume more than one role.

One usually distinguishes between five kinds of resources:

- Personnel
- Materials
- Utilities
- Database
- Application

Furthermore, "internal" and "external" resources are differentiated. Internet access, for example, provided by an Internet Service Provider (ISP), is an external resource. Resources can be assigned to more than one organization unit, but there can be only one unit to which they are disciplinarily subordinate.

By a *role*, an activity profile (or a "position") is meant which is necessary for the execution of activities. When carrying out these activities, roles are taken over by the respective resources.

With an allocation of resources to roles as part of a modeling, it will be documented which resource will be designated for which role (as a primary allocation or as a substitute). By assigning roles to the activities of the various process models, it will be documented who is involved in the various process flows. Therefore, it will be noted which roles (and thus indirectly which resources) are required for the execution of the activities. Since several resources come into question for the perception of a role, a direct allocation of resources to activities is not meaningful. If necessary, the respectively available resource will be used.

3.6   Case Study

In this section, the concepts and modeling languages previously explained are illustrated with a running example. In particular, the process of acquiring new customers up to the delivery of a product will be modeled. For a comprehensive and formal description of this process with the relevant aspects, process models at different hierarchical levels, object models and organization models are used. A key point that is characterized by the Horus method described in Chap. 4 is the integration of various concepts, which is particularly evident in the detailed analysis of the XML nets used.

The procedure model shown in Fig. 3.30 shows the process from acquisition to delivery, initially at a high level of abstraction. Activity Acquisition represents the ongoing contact with customers and prospects, ideally leading to an interest in a product. An acquisition in practice itself is a complex process, of course, that

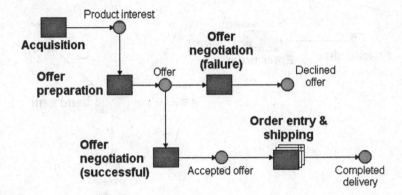

Fig. 3.30 Process model—from acquisition to delivery

is, subject to many rules and often binds the most expensive resources as well. In our case study, we will intentionally abstract from this complexity—only a single box is used—knowing that acquisition processes often open up the most interesting potential for inherent optimization. Upon interest in certain products of the product line, an offer is created and negotiated. An unsuccessful negotiation leads to the rejection of the offer. If successful, the offer will be accepted, with amendments if necessary. After acceptance of the offer by the customer, the order is created in the last activity `Order entry and shipping` of the described core process, so that a shipment of the desired item can be carried out.

This process step is refined and is described at a more detailed level in the procedure model shown in Fig. 3.31. A new order is documented by a sales clerk based on the acceptance of the offer. The items to be delivered under the context of the contract are then sent by a shipping clerk. An inventory update is carried out in the context of the shipping process.

In Fig. 3.32, the relevant organization model for the process is presented, firstly in the form of an organization chart. On the other hand, roles will be required as an additional element for a full description within the framework of the organization model which can then be assigned to individual process steps. Roles are assigned at the second level in the represented process example, that is, in the refinement of the activity `Order entry and shipping`. For this purpose, the roles of `Sales clerk` and `Shipping clerk` are used as represented in Fig. 3.31. A modeling of single resources and its assignment to roles or the organizational units represented in the organizational structure diagram will be renounced in this example. The rhombi in Fig. 3.32 symbolize each of the hierarchical aggregation relationships of the hierarchically subordinate to the hierarchically primary organization unit, respectively.

Figure 3.33 illustrates the aspects that can be formally modeled and their interrelationships of the XML net used in this example. Also, the processing of the object structures and the organizational settlement are hereby described next to the pure sequence of the process through the correlation to the roles.

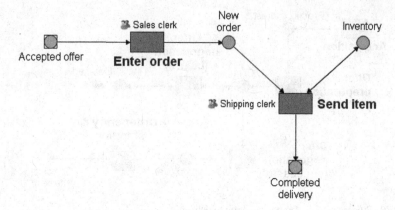

Fig. 3.31 Refinement—Order entry and shipping

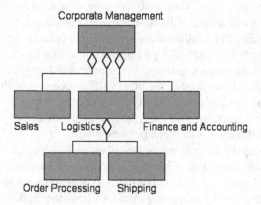

Fig. 3.32 Organization structure relevant to the process in Fig. 3.31

The filtering schemes are described with pseudo code in the example shown. Filtering scheme FS_1 retrieves the offers from the object store Accepted offer. This will ensure that they are in the status Commissioned, and therefore may be further processed. One order each will be applied to the item selected by the activity Enter order. With the acquisition of an order, filtering scheme FS_2 creates new orders where the order number is generated, the articles and the customer are acquired from the offer and the status of the newly created order is initially set to Open. Filtering scheme FS_3 is used to determine the order items. Before shipping an article over the activity, Ship item can be carried out, it will be determined over inscription I of the activity Ship item whether a sufficient stock of items is available in the warehouse so that a delivery of the number of articles ordered can be carried out. Following the execution, that is, the firing of the activity, updates of the inventory over the filtering scheme FS_5 as well as the integration of deliveries into the customer's transaction data over the filtering scheme FS_6 are conducted.

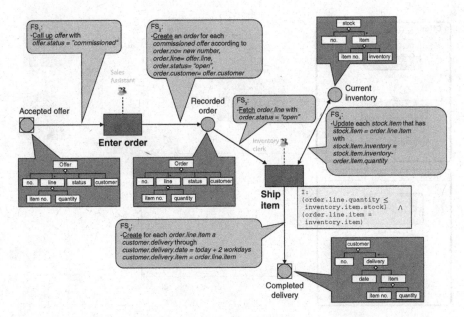

Fig. 3.33 XML net refinement—aspects and coherencies

The assigned objects can be described with the object model shown in Fig. 3.34. From this, the business object structures used in the XML net can be created and used directly. `Offer` and `Order` can be represented directly by the use of the respective aggregation of the same name, that is, the complex business object, for example. The business object structures for `Inventory` and `Delivery` could also be created by defining a complex business object. For example, the XML structure for `Delivery` can be created by the aggregation of the objects `Customer`, `Delivery`, and `Item`.

3.7 Self Control

Exercise 3.1. Model the core processes of an electrical power company in a liberalized electricity market. The provider has no capacity for in-house generation and purchases its energy entirely on the European Power Exchange. The main tasks in the enterprise are marketing, customer acquisition, individual pricing and profitability, customer-specific load forecast and total load forecasting, organization of the network transmission, purchase of electricity, advance payment determination as well as customer billing, controlling, administration, and staff. Particularly suitable for automation are the processes in setting up a customer supply. In each case, two sides must be considered: customer service, or service and allocation of resources. Outsourcing will be used for marketing and staff.

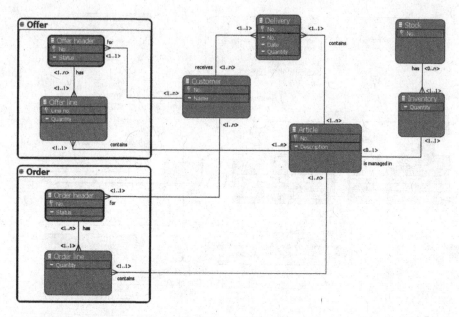

Fig. 3.34 Object model—Order entry and shipping

Exercise 3.2. Model a traffic light which can change from red directly to green, from green to yellow and from yellow back to red (e.g., traffic lights of this type are used in the Netherlands or in New Zealand). Two such traffic lights are to be used at an intersection; these traffic lights must be synchronized so that traffic is not unnecessarily obstructed.

Initially model a simple synchronization, by which the intersection is safe in the sense that both traffic lights will never switch to green at the same time; it may occur, however, that one of the two sets of traffic lights rarely or never will turn green.

Then model a more refined synchronization, by which the intersection is not only safe but also that the streets in question are treated fairly in the sense that the two traffic lights will alternately turn green.

Exercise 3.3. If a credit application has been made, it will initially undergo a careful review. This examination can lead to a denial of the application. The customer will be informed of the denial and a copy of the cancellation is filed with the bank. If the application is approved, the customer will receive the requested credit after conclusion of the contract.

- Create a procedure model.
- Model the business process Loan Processing. Take into account that the customer may apply for the loan via the Internet, via letter, or via fax.
- Refine the activity by which the contract will be concluded. Present in the refinement that the application is sent to the customer and that he signs and

returns this to you. The contract is archived and a copy is sent to the customer after the countersigning by the credit committee.

- Refine the review of the credit application. Rename object store `Application examined` to `Application approved`. Connect both object stores directly to the refinement of the review of the credit application in the event of a denial.

It should be noted that this is an example in which models are made possible by refinements, which would otherwise lead to a contradiction in the model. Without the refinement, the application would be simultaneously approved and rejected in this case.

When reviewing the credit application, the following business rules will continue to be applied:

1. If the credit amount applied for is greater than two monthly salaries, a denial is then carried out automatically.
2. If the relationship to the customer has not yet existed sufficiently long, a denial will also be the result.

For applications that do not comply with rule 1 or rule 2, it will be reviewed whether the customer past payment history was good. If this is not the case (internal black list), a denial will be the result. Credit applications where the sum is less than 0.5 of a monthly salary will be approved automatically, however. If the sum is smaller than one month's salary, the responsible clerk can then decide whether the application will be granted or not. The credit committee will decide on credit sums which are greater than a monthly salary.

- Model the corresponding processes.
- Model an adequately structured application form as an object type.
- Model an additional object-type `Credit application` in a new information model and add suitable attributes for this.
- Describe a possible exemplary organizational structure of the enterprise.
- Define resources suitable for the organizational model developed. Model both human and technical resources (material resources) and also take the cost rates into account. Also model the suitable roles.
- Assign appropriate roles to the activities in the model `Complete contract`.

Exercise 3.4. Van der Aalst et al. suggest comparing the power of modeling methods (and workflow systems) based on (workflow) patterns. Such patterns are abstractions of concrete modeling constructs that occur in practice in different contexts. Individually it concerns the following patterns:

(a) *Basic Control Flow Patterns*: Simple constructs that are supported by nearly all modeling languages.

- *Sequence*: B follows A if A was completed.
- *Parallel Split*: If A is complete, then B and C can be run in parallel (B and C are then placed in the condition "execute ready").
- *Synchronization*: C can be started when A and B are complete.

- *Exclusive Choice*: Dependent upon a condition, either B or C follows A.
- *Simple Merge* C is executable if A or B was completed.

(b) *Advanced Branching and Synchronization Patterns*: In practice, common, simple constructs that are, however, not directly supported by all modeling languages.

- *Multi-choice*: After A follows, depending on a condition, only B or only C, or B and C.
- *Synchronizing Merge*: C can be started if A and B are complete and if A and B were simultaneously executable. Otherwise, C can be started if only A or B is complete and if only A or B were executable. C is executed only once.
- *Multi-merge*: A can be started each time B or C is complete. Overall, therefore, A can be started twice if both B and C were activated.
- *Discriminator*: X can be started if *n* of *m* direct preceding activities have been completed to X. Altogether, X is executed once.

(c) *Structural Patterns*: In practice common but often not supported by all modeling languages. Emulation of such structures in languages that do not support this are inclined to result in confusing, complicated models. In some cases, emulation is not possible.

- *Arbitrary Cycles*: Unstructured cycles, similar to a GOTO in classic programming languages, which can have multiple cycle entry or cycle exit points.
- *Implicit Termination*: A (sub-) process is to end automatically if no further activities can be executed.

(d) *Patterns Involving Multiple Instances*: Patterns as they typically occur in the processing of hierarchical objects (such as orders with order items). Only few modeling languages tend to support these patterns directly and completely.

- *Multiple Instances Without Synchronization*: B is started several times in parallel, with respect to various business objects after A has been completed. Synchronization of various B is not required.
- *Multiple Instances with a Priori Design Time Knowledge*: B is always launched exactly *n* times (specification in the model), in parallel with respect to *n* business objects, after A has been completed. C is started after all B have been completed.
- *Multiple Instances with a Priori Runtime Knowledge*: B is always launched dependent on A (at runtime) exactly *n* times, parallel with respect to *n* business objects, after A has been completed. C is started after all B have been completed.
- *Multiple Instances Without a Priori Runtime Knowledge*: B is started with respect to a business object after A has been completed. Before B is stopped, it can be determined, under certain circumstances, that a new B must be executed in parallel with another business object. C is started after all B have been completed.

(e) *State-Based Patterns*: The execution of an activity is contingent on the state of other activities. Directly supported by only a few modeling languages.

- *Deferred Choice*: Once A has been completed, both B and C can be executed. At the execution of B, C is disabled and vice versa. The decision as to which of the two activities is executed is determined by external factors.
- *Interleaved Parallel Routing*: Several activities are to be executed where the order does not matter. However, only one of the activities may at most be in process at any given time.
- *Milestone*: The activity B can only then be executed (but need not be executed) if A is complete and C is not yet completed.

(f) *Cancelation Patterns*: Termination of activities and their follow-up activities.

- *Cancel Activity*: An activity which is execution ready, or is already in execution, is deactivated or stopped.
- *Cancel Case*: An entire process and all its activities are completely deactivated or aborted.

Present these samples graphically in Petri net notations and discuss the following theses:

- Samples are missing for problem definitions, such as resource allocation, case treatment, exception handling, and transaction management.
- Almost all current modeling tools support the Basic Control Flow Patterns; the advanced patterns, by contrast, are only supported in part or not at all.
- Prior to the acquisition of a modeling tool, it should be ascertained which patterns are common in the enterprise. Unnecessary costs can therefore be avoided by adapting a "wrong" system to the available patterns.

3.8 Bibliographical References and Web Links

As already mentioned in Chap. 1, the preoccupation with business processes, their analysis and improvement goes back to Hammer and Champy (1993). The dissertation by Petri (1962) laid the foundation for the Petri-net-based modeling tool used here. A modern introduction to the subject is Reisig (2011).

XML nets go back to the so-called *SGML nets* from the dissertation by Weitz (1999). They were described in detail in the dissertation of Lenz (2002); see also Lenz and Oberweis (2003).

The Entity-Relationship model goes back to the work of Chen (1976). It is today's standard in conceptual database design, see, for example, Silberschatz et al. (2010). The AOM model or Asset-Oriented Modeling is described by Daum (2003). For an introduction to modeling with UML, see, for example, Rosenberg and Stephens (2007) or Podeswa (2009). The relationship between process, data, and organizational modeling is also presented by Scheer (2000a,b) and Scheer et al. (2002).

A comprehensive collection of material on the topic of Petri nets can be found in the "World of Petri nets" which is maintained at the University of Hamburg, see www.informatik.uni-hamburg.de/TGI/PetriNets/.

As a preparatory reading for Exercise 3.4, we recommend reading the paper by Van der Aalst (2003) on Workflow Patterns.

Chapter 4
The Horus Method

Petri nets are impressive in business process modeling due to the simplicity of the graphical presentation in connection with their expressive power. One can achieve a high precision of models, and the operational semantics allows formal for analysis and dynamic simulation. Practice shows, however, that a powerful modeling language alone is not enough: Users require guidance and assistance in the preparation of models, that is, during *application* of the language. They seek recipe-like guidelines that have been proven in practice. To this extent, a modeling language is only as good as the method that shows the way to its successful use.

In this book, we employ the Horus® Method[TM1], featured in this chapter. It defines various stages of modeling but is not intended as a replacement for comprehensive procedure models, such as ones for the development of business information systems or for business process reengineering. Instead, it is designed to be easily embedded into procedure models. In Chap. 5, this will be described for different areas of application.

4.1 Principles of the Horus Method

Many methods for business process modeling consider the modeling of process procedures as an isolated step. Still, other methods may take different aspects of a process into account (procedure, organization structure, business rules, etc.), yet they still model these isolated from one another. For the representation of an as-is process, this might be acceptable—for an optimization and redesign of processes; however, this is not suitable. Here, an integrated analysis of all aspects relevant to the process is indispensable. Thus, for example, even the most sophisticated procedure will only deliver suboptimal process results when not all necessary business objects are available in a sufficient quality standard.

---

[1] The Horus® Method[TM] is a product of Horus software GmbH, Ettlingen, Germany.

F. Schönthaler et al., *Business Processes for Business Communities*,
DOI 10.1007/978-3-642-24791-0_4, © Springer-Verlag Berlin Heidelberg 2012

The Horus method solves this problem by always looking at a process together with its organizational environment or context. This applies to both the modeling described in this section as well as to the optimization and further use of the resulting models. In addition, this method motivates a user to describe all relevant aspects with exactly those techniques that are best suited for them. This, at first, may sound trivial but is a problem frequently found in practice. The expert will immediately recognize whether a model was created by a specialist in object modeling or a Petri net specialist or by an organizational structure manager. The specialist will always try to describe as many aspects as possible in the modeling language familiar to her or him as in the case of an object modeler, for example. He or she will try to place very many procedural aspects concerning specializations and integrity constraints in the object model. The Horus method provides a solution by guiding a user with clearly defined steps through the modeling process, giving instructions as to what essential facts need to be modeled in which particular manner.

4.1.1   How to Apply the Modeling Language

The Horus method offers steps both for model expansion through additional elements (activities, organization units, etc.) as well as for joining various modeling elements (e.g., organization unit is responsible for an activity or executes it).

Figure 4.1 provides an overview of the Horus method. Horus subdivides business process engineering into four phases. Phase 0 is the *preparation* of the engineering project. Phase 1 is the *strategy and architecture* phase to study the strategic aspects

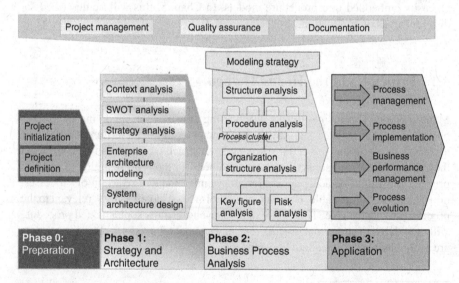

Fig. 4.1 Structure and steps of the Horus method

and definition of enterprise and system architecture. Phase 2 is the detailed *business process analysis*. Phase 3 is the subsequent *usage* of the model. Beyond these phases, modeling is accompanied by *project management*, measures for *quality assurance*, and up-to-date *documentation*.

Project definition creation takes place together with the initialization of the project during the preparation phase. This determines which parts of an organization will be examined—often called *project scope*—and what budget and time frames are available for this purpose. Project goals to be accomplished are additionally outlined and examined regarding their strategic and economic value, including a subsequent budget comparison. Phases 1 and 2 build the core of Horus modeling and will be discussed below in detail. They deal with the analysis and modeling of strategic aspects associated with the business and system architecture, as well as a detailed examination of the business processes. A special feature of the Petri nets used here is their simulation capability. In practice, simulation proves itself as an instrument for the dynamic analysis and testing of models "under load." Simulation results can be visualized in a simple, understandable, and meaningful form by way of graphic animations. When, to which extent, and with which intensity the simulation will be used has to be clarified on an individual basis with regard to cost and benefit aspects. Further information on this can be found in Sect. 4.4.

The attainable uses of a Horus business process model go far beyond high-quality documentation. They extend from knowledge management to process implementation and business performance management to process evolution. The different applications of the Horus models shall not be considered further at this point; they are the subject of Sect. 4.5.

4.1.2 Abstraction Principle

Before examining the various steps of the Horus method more thoroughly, it is important to understand the basic principles of the method. Its comprehension will substantially facilitate an application of the method as well as a subsequent interpretation of the modeling results. The principles also make modeling appear difficult for some users, so that specific training measures must be applied at this point if necessary.

The most important principle of the Horus method is *abstraction*. It denotes a thought process with respect to specific objects of reality, where general and specific properties are separated from one another to then depict the generally valid properties in a more general or simpler theoretical model. This conceptual model is, in our case, the Horus business process model.

Abstraction at first sight is a simple, natural process. Children master and apply it intuitively and successfully with ease. Upon seeing a trunk in a confusing picture, they easily construe an elephant. Adults often have problems with this. They lose themselves in details and are often not in a position to recognize the really important and generally valid facts and issues. In modeling, this can lead to seemingly insurmountable difficulties and, ultimately, to an essentially simple modeling technique being rejected as too complex and completely inappropriate. Then the call for additional and particularly specific modeling elements arises, which in many cases is merely a work-around to preclude a forced abstraction.

For these reasons, the Horus method is equipped with various techniques to simplify abstraction. It consciously includes steps that start, for example, in the procedure analysis phase (see Sect. 4.3.2) with easily communicated specific use cases or business events, then gradually rises them to a higher level of abstraction, that is, into the target model. The Horus tools also facilitate abstraction, by offering the possibility to place specific examples behind each model element, that is, objects of the real world. Indeed, for an understanding of object type `Customer order`, it is simply the easiest when the customer order screen or the scanned order document is displayed upon pressing a button.

Can the thought processes, which come up during abstraction, be classified? Typical operations here are *generalization*, which seeks general attributes in objects or object types, forming an object type from these at a higher level of abstraction. The inverse of generalization is *specialization*. The generalized object type then inherits its attributes to the more specific object types. Another operation type is *aggregation*, which combines different types of objects to a new object type on a higher level of abstraction. The opposite of aggregation is deaggregation or *decomposition*. Finally, there is *grouping*, which forms a new object type at a higher level from the combination of several similar types of objects. Here, the inversion is *degrouping*.

Techniques that use these abstractions directly find application in the Horus method for a variety of modeling aspects. The Horus method offers, besides abstraction, broader forms of structuring which are described in the following.

4.1.3 Structuring Principle

Structuring is a fundamental principle that is a recurrent theme in the Horus method. Structuring creates the possibility to model even large-scale systems in a detailed yet comprehensive and understandable manner. On the one hand, this is achieved by describing facts and circumstances of different types with the most appropriate languages in different submodels, which can then be connected to one another through well-defined links. If the processing of outerwear is carried out, for example, in the same manner for men's and women's clothing, then the differences between these products find themselves only in the object model, while uniform workflows are defined in the procedure model with corresponding links to the various object types.

A lack of structuring capability is, in addition to a lack of abstraction capability, one of the most common causes of acceptance problems during modeling. A user often complains about confusing models and too high a complexity. He or she then pleads for a focus on a few important facts, which in many cases he or she is not even able to properly identify. The Horus modeling languages therefore provide practical, simple, and easy-to-use structuring techniques. Important roles are taken on by refinement, decomposition, and clustering; a structuring character is also inherent to the abstractions mentioned above. Further discussions concerning these techniques can be found in the following sections.

Two equally important structuring techniques, which should be part of the capacity of a modeler and which can be found in the context of the Horus method in different variants, shall be examined next.

4.1.3.1 Perspectives of the Balanced Scorecard

The *Balanced Scorecard* (BSc), introduced in 1992 by Kaplan and Norton, has meanwhile become a popular management tool. It is used to measure a company's performance based on meaningful key indicators, known as so-called *key* or *business performance indicators* (KPIs or BPIs, respectively). The distinguishing feature of the BSc—in contrast to traditional key indicator systems that focus exclusively on financial indicators—is that the indicators assign different perspectives, which include the actual performance process as well as future potential. Thus, BSc overcomes the problem that only a past consideration of financial key indicators is made possible per se, finding limited use for foresighted enterprise management.

Although the perspectives of the BSc are freely selectable for each organization, some typical perspectives have become clear in practice:

- Finances
- Customers
- Internal processes
- Potentials (human capital, innovation, regeneration, and growth)

As in the BSc, these perspectives are also used in the Horus method as an expressive structuring instrument. They are used to classify objectives, strategies, key figures, and risks, thus bringing structure and order into initially extemporaneously confusing models. In addition, they also serve as a template to ensure that no perspectives are excluded from consideration. The results are more complete and thus higher quality models.

4.1.3.2 Strategy and Tactics

In practice, objectives, strategies, and risks are often classified in terms of their maturity. One makes a distinction between long-, medium- and short-term nature, using the performed classification for the structuring of appropriate models. This may be a beneficial and easily applied instrument for objectives; for strategies and risks or even key figures, however, the economic significance is missing, which makes handling much more difficult.

In contrast, the Horus method prefers a distinction between strategy, tactics, and operational business as follows:

- *Strategy*: Strategies focus on long-term measures or sets of measures, which are carefully planned and systematically pursued to achieve a business objective. During strategic planning, this involves breaking down the corporate mission into business objectives, thereby operationalizing them by way of appropriate key figures.
- *Tactics*: Tactics determine ways and means to achieve medium-range objectives. In tactical planning, medium-range strategies are developed, evaluated, and brought into connection with the enterprise business process network. Planning will view the processes holistically, taking place in a cross-process manner.
- *Operational business*: In contrast, short-term planning in the context of individual business processes takes place during operative planning. Planning is carried out mainly at a clerical level and is a component of the business processes themselves, that is, it is mirrored again in individual business activities.

Strategic aspects clearly stand in the foreground during the strategy and architecture phase (Phase 1, see Sect. 4.2) of the Horus method. Strategic business objectives, strategic risks, and strategic key figures are modeled here. In simple terms, the defined strategies are the key element of modeling. All submodels are set in relation to the strategies and focus on an optimal implementation of these strategies.

Tactical issues are central to the business process analysis (Phase 2, see Sect. 4.3). The procedures that form the core of every tactic, in connection with the organizational structure and the business objects, are the key element of this phase. This then deals with the tactical risks, which show the threats for the tactics and the tactical key performance figures, which measure the performance and success of the tactics. With the Horus tool, tactical objectives can be modeled. The Horus method does not recommend the use of tactical objectives, however, since its use is limited mostly in the context of the modeling and hardly justifies the modeling effort.

4.2   Phase 1: From a Mission to an Architecture Model

The primary goals of the Horus method are the gathering and structuring of business requirements as well as the creation of a comprehensive business process model under consideration of all relevant aspects including the process background and context. The focus therefore lies on the actual *model development* and not on process improvement, the development of an information system, or even the enforcement of the process within the organization. Such tasks will be dealt with and solved in Chap. 5 by embedding the Horus method into comprehensive procedure models such as business process reengineering.

Nevertheless, the Horus method puts an analysis of a company's strategy as well as the modeling of the corporate structure and the architecture of a supporting information system at the beginning of a business process analysis. The reason is that it has shown in practice that only in this way it is possible to involve decision makers adequately in a modeling project and to convince them of ongoing cooperation and support. Ultimately, this concerns the analysis of the client's expectations to business process engineering and the results that can be achieved with it. In addition, it concerns aligning these expectations, which can change often and quickly in the course of the project, with the results of the project.

Figure 4.2 shows details of the approach in Phase 1 of the Horus method in a Petri net representation. The Petri net places the activities in a logical order and describes how the results of an activity will continue to be used in subsequent activities. However, the net is not to be confused with a waterfall model as is still widely used in information system or software development. In contrast, activities may need to go through several cycles or be eliminated in some cases completely. It should be noted that some of the activities are refined: context analysis, strategy analysis, and modeling of the enterprise architecture. The corresponding refinement nets can be found in subsequent sections below. They also show the use of the model types created in Phase 1. In addition to use in Phase 1 activities, the models in their entirety form the result of the strategy and architecture phase, which is the starting point for all activities in Phase 2.

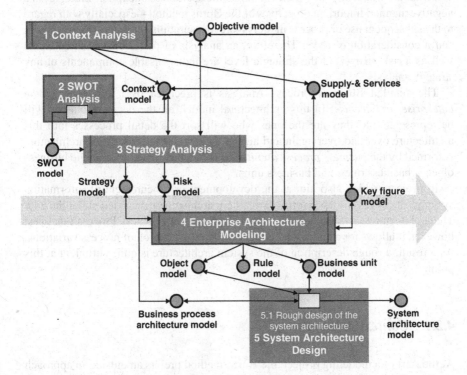

Fig. 4.2 Procedure model of the strategy and analysis phase (Phase 1)

An important goal of the strategy and architecture phase is to establish a reliable framework for the subsequent analysis and modeling of the relevant business processes. Basis of the consideration is the project definition acquired and adopted during the preparation phase, in connection with the corporate mission that manifests itself in a so-called mission statement and which should be the overall project driver. The initial steps to be gone through are summarized under the term *context analysis* and describe the environment or context of the modeling project.

Within the scope given by the context analysis, a SWOT analysis will investigate the *strengths*, *weaknesses*, *opportunities*, and *threats* for the enterprise. The results are relevant for the focal areas of subsequent analytical activities. Although a SWOT analysis is not an immediate prerequisite for a strategy analysis, we do recommend not to abdicate this option. It helps to avoid unnecessarily detailed analysis and, on the other hand, ensures that important analysis fields with high optimization potential are not neglected.

The *strategy analysis* itself delivers details regarding the strategies pursued within the enterprise and establishes cohesion and relationships between these. Existing interactions between strategies will be identified. This is especially interesting when strategies are also observed that are not defined explicitly as such. Implicit strategies are frequently identified that affect the usefulness of explicit strategies in a negative manner. Important objectives of the Horus method—especially with regard to the subsequent use of process models—are measurability of process performance and a consideration of risks. Therefore, an analysis of performance indicators as well as a risk analysis at the strategic level are indispensable components of any strategy analysis.

The detailed Business Process Analysis is preceded by a *modeling of the enterprise architecture*. In this architectural model, all the decision makers will be represented, as they are the ones who will sort the detail processes into this architecture over and over again and again. The core of the enterprise architecture is formed by the *business process architecture*, which is linked to strategic business objects, business rules, and business units.

In projects which also aim at the development or procurement of information systems, the design of the information system architecture is carried out at the end. The architecture has little influence on the subsequent Business Process Analysis; however, it allows for a value- and budget-oriented evaluation of process variations. As a result, a rough description of the system architecture is quite sufficient at this point.

4.2.1 Context Analysis

At the start of a modeling project, the Horus method prefers an outside-in approach by first defining and analyzing the environment of the system to be modeled. This drives home a framework which serves as a fixed and usually unchangeable reference point within the modeling project. In practice, it can be observed that this

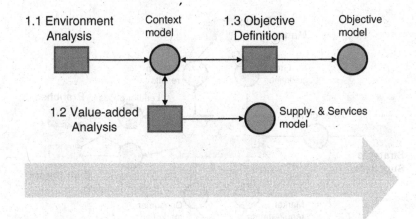

Fig. 4.3 Procedure model of context analysis (refinement of Step 1 from Phase 1)

reference point will be referred to repeatedly by decision makers. Figure 4.3 shows the stages of the context analysis as well as which model elements are then produced and processed.

4.2.1.1 Environment Analysis

Following the outside-in approach, during the *environment analysis*, the external influence factors are analyzed first, which affect the contemplated system and often even the entire enterprise. It is important to recognize and evaluate their mutual ramifications and dependencies. In most cases, this assessment is limited to qualitative aspects. However, enterprises are now increasingly at the mercy of external protagonists—we are talking about *external entities*—and the enterprises have no other choice than to prepare their internal processes for a rapid response to external influences. Practitioners like to fall back on simulation in such cases to run through various scenarios in order to quantitatively identify dependencies and ramifications.

Figure 4.4 shows a sample result of an environment analysis, that is, the context model of the leather goods division of a trading company. It is interesting to note that the group management stands outside of the observed system and is consequently regarded as an external entity. Branch offices that, in a sense, are sister entities of the leather goods division are seen—as with the external distributors—as external entities. It is clear that abstraction is required in the environment analysis so that only very important external entities are taken into account and that a summary of the entities is also carried out to generic entities.

The context model shown depicts typical external entities as they are repeatedly found in practice. Other typical entities (influencing factors in parentheses) are investors (capital), labor (workers), society (values, rules), environment (natural resources), or raw material suppliers.

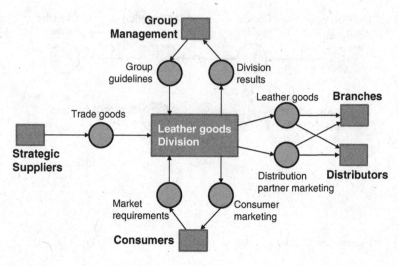

Fig. 4.4 Context model of the leather goods division

In Fig. 4.4, it stands out that the consumers are considered an external entity, yet no products are delivered to them. More specifically, the connection between retail outlets and distributors to the retail customers is missing. The reason is that this (in reality) existing connection lies beyond the system context. If the order and supply relationships are to be analyzed, they must be included with the system context.

In conclusion, it should be noted that the context model is depicted here in standard Petri net representation. In practice, however, reference is often made to a presentation enriched with icons and informal depiction elements, which are part of the functionality of Horus tools.

4.2.1.2   Added-Value Analysis

The modeling framework to be spanned during context analysis includes a definition of the *supply and services portfolio* of the system under consideration, that is, the leather goods division in the example shown in Fig. 4.5. Products and services are contained within the supply and services model that ultimately constitutes the added value of the enterprise. With regard to the context analysis, intermediate products which already include an added value are not taken into account here. It can make sense, however, to model intermediate products in the context of the subsequent business process analysis—to motivate a tactical product driven penetration of new markets, for example—to refine the supply and services model.

Generalizations as well as groupings and aggregations are implemented for the creation of the supply and services model, in order to depict the added value structure as realistically as possible. A product range is modeled in Fig. 4.5 where

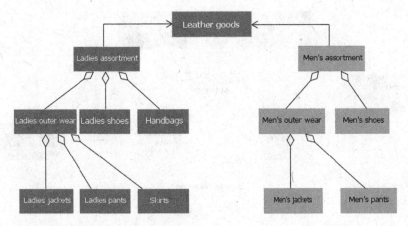

Fig. 4.5 Supply and services model of the leather goods division

aggregations can be primarily found. Generalizations and in some cases groupings can be found with further refinement of the portfolio, however.

When modeling using Horus, links between the elements of different submodels can be established. The method provides for syntactic correctness of these references, where the semantics are well defined for each reference allowed. References are exclusively established to external entities in the context model during supply and services modeling. This specifies that the referenced external entity is the recipient of the service or the performance supplier. In this case, the performance would be a performance bought in addition.

4.2.1.3 Objectives Definition

With the context model and the supply and services model, the width of the analysis and modeling activity can be demarcated. These models are complemented by the *objectives model*, which delivers important references for estimating the required depth of detail necessary in specific analysis areas.

During the strategy and architecture phase, strategic business objectives are defined in the objectives model. They are derived from the enterprise mission, then broken down through specialization until they span a complete objective area for the system to be examined. One speaks of a complete objective area when all issues addressed in the mission statement have been mapped into suitable objectives. Figure 4.6 shows an example of an objectives model for the leather goods division.

High-quality objectives models should formulate goals at different levels of abstraction. This is the only way to prevent decision makers from losing themselves in objective details whose meaning they can often not even understand. On the other hand, it must be ensured that the objectives models can also be interpreted

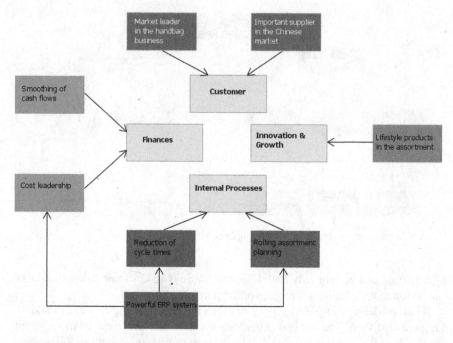

Fig. 4.6 Objectives model of the leather goods division

by business users, whereby the detail objectives will help in this regard. Figure 4.6 depicts how these requirements can be elegantly solved by way of specialization hierarchies. As an example, the goal to have a powerful ERP system models multiple objectives simultaneously, as a specialization at a higher level of abstraction. The example clearly shows that the specialization should not be confused with a decomposition. Specialization has to provide a transition to a lower level of abstraction, not to break a goal down into subgoals. In this respect, parallel goals will always exist in an objectives model, with or without specialization.

Completeness is an important quality factor of an objectives model. However, completeness cannot be formally proven, which is why it has turned out to be reasonable not to speak of completeness but of the *balance* of an objectives model. An objectives model is then in balance (or balanced) if it takes all perspectives of an enterprise into account. We therefore recommend that objectives models, as they are being created, be aligned to the four perspectives discussed in Sect. 4.1.3 in connection with the model structure. They go back to the above-mentioned Balanced Scorecard. In Fig. 4.6, the generic objectives defined for this are *finances*, *customers*, *internal processes*, as well as *innovation and growth*, broken down gradually by means of specialization.

In objectives modeling, references to external entities are established in the context model in order to document which of these entities specifically refer to an objective. In other words, it is demonstrated which external entity positively or negatively influences the objective, or which external entity is influenced in a particular manner by reaching the objective.

4.2.2 SWOT Analysis

Still following an outside-in approach, context analysis is succeeded by a first management-oriented *enterprise analysis*. This is deliberately not organized as a formal process, but in many cases it is more like a brainstorming session. Decision makers and opinion leaders first exchange their thoughts on the strengths and weaknesses of the company. After such an analysis of the internal influencing factors, they allocate the external factors by addressing opportunities and/or threats for the enterprise. This analysis technology is known as *SWOT analysis*, see the notes above for Fig. 4.2.

Figure 4.7 shows an example of a SWOT model of the leather goods division. Known abstraction hierarchies are used for the depiction. Abstractions are carried out with multistage specialization hierarchies in this case. Primarily they serve to differentiate between internal and external factors and then to classify the variables in strengths, weaknesses, opportunities and threats. Either way it is clear that weaknesses frequently can also be strengths, for example, highly specialized

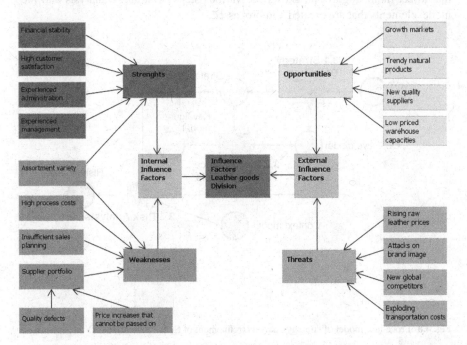

Fig. 4.7 SWOT model of the leather goods division

machinery with which large market shares can be gained, but are quite uneconomic for standard orders. Alternatively, the chance of entering the Chinese market also poses new risk potentials. Although different views can be explained in detailed descriptions, it is recommended anyway to separate strengths and weaknesses or opportunities and threats through naming, such as the distinction between the highly specialized machinery for special production as a strength from an overly strong highly specialized machinery for standard orders as a weakness. In the present example, a further specialization of the factors according to the perspectives of the Balanced Scorecard were dispensed with, whereby such structures can very well be encountered from case to case in practice.

For improved traceability of SWOT analysis results, it is common practice to establish references between influence factors and external entities within the context model. These references determine which external entity is responsible for the influence factor or which they affect.

4.2.3   Strategy Analysis

In the context of the *strategy analysis*, strategies are defined in conjunction with associated performance indicators to measure their effectiveness as well as the risks that affect them. Figure 4.8 shows the various steps of strategy analysis and the model elements that are created and processed.

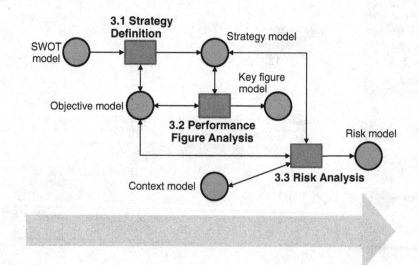

Fig. 4.8 Procedure model of strategy analysis (refinement of Step 3 from Phase 1)

4.2.3.1 Strategy Definition

The most important starting point for strategy definition is the *objectives model*. For each of the objectives, considerations have to be taken into account as to which strategies are suitable to achieve the desired goal within the predetermined period of time and within the given budget. There will also be strategies which influence more than one objective. It must be determined whether each influence is positive or negative in nature. In practice, these correlation considerations often lead to strategies being discarded due to their negative side effects, even though they have a positive effect on individual objectives.

Figure 4.9 shows the strategy model of the leather goods division in the known representation in the form of abstraction hierarchies. It nicely shows how here again that structuring has been carried out with respect to the perspectives of the Balanced Scorecard. Abstraction is achieved through aggregation and generalization hierarchies. An interesting modeling case is the development of the purse business, for which the two substrategies Price promotions for handbags and Lifestyle products have been modeled. Lifestyle products itself is a major strategy that is assigned to both customer perspective as well as the

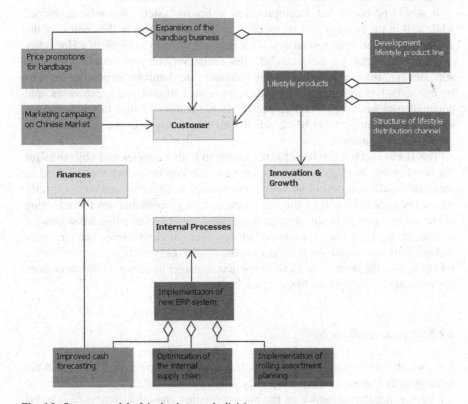

Fig. 4.9 Strategy model of the leather goods division

innovation and growth perspective. `Improved cash forecasting` is also worth mentioning, which is both a substrategy of an ERP implementation as well as the main strategy from a financial perspective.

The motivation for developing a strategy is always the pursuit of a business objective. In strategy modeling, references are therefore built up to the goals of the objectives model. However, it must be specified in each case whether an objective will be affected in a positive or negative manner by the strategy. Especially the negative influences have to be considered particularly in line with the model analysis (see the comments above regarding the correlation considerations).

4.2.3.2 Analysis of Performance Figures

Clearly, it is not enough to define strategies only; there must also be possibilities to measure their effectiveness. Suitable are so-called *performance indicators*. These are key figures that define how, at what times, and how often they are measured. Minimum and maximum values, tolerances, and thresholds are then specified. Performance indicators measure the intensity and quality of strategy implementation and the contribution that the strategy delivers for goal attainment.

It should be noted that a complete key indicator system cannot be developed while still in the strategy and architecture phase—this occurs in the context of the subsequent business process analysis (see Sect. 4.3.4 for an example of a Horus key figure model)—but that the focus here lies exclusively on performance indicators with strategic relevance. Financial key indicators are dominant in practice but will be increasingly supplemented by indicators related to customers, processes, and potential perspectives. In this respect, it is recommended that the performance indicators at strategic level be classified correspondingly with the perspectives of the Balanced Scorecard.

The Horus method provides for references to both strategies and objectives for the key figures. Strategy references define which key indicators will be used to measure the effectiveness of strategy implementation. *Objective references* specify which key indicators will be used to measure strategy contributions for achieving the respective goal. It is obvious that these two forms of referencing are somewhat redundant. In many cases, it should suffice, for example, to reference strategies and implicitly determine the references to the objectives from the strategy-objective relations. It is the responsibility of the project manager to demand references from key indicators to objectives, to strategies, or both.

4.2.3.3 Risk Analysis

Risks which may jeopardize the success of an enterprise have to be addressed in the Strategy and Analysis phase as well. They pose a threat to objective achievement and can have a negative influence on the implementation and effectiveness of selected strategies. The importance of a risk analysis is not to be underestimated, as it lays the foundation for an efficient risk management. The Horus method already provides the first steps for a risk analysis in the SWOT analysis. The primary objective of the SWOT analysis is to integrate an enterprise's management and, together with it, to consider threats to the enterprise, among other issues. In contrast, risk analysis considers risks in a much more detail, providing a formal structure in the risk model where the risks are arranged at different levels of abstraction. The Balanced Scorecard perspectives are also used in many practical applications to structure the risk model.

Risk analysis still does not deliver a complete risk model as part of the Strategy and Architecture phase, but instead, focuses on *strategic* risks. This refers to those risks defined at the same level of abstraction as strategies and business objectives. A complete and detailed risk model arises only within the context of the subsequent business process analysis (see Sect. 4.3.5 for an example of a Horus risk model).

References in context, objective, and strategy models can be built from risk models. With this, the external entities responsible for the risk or vulnerable to the risk will be defined. By referencing strategies and objectives, it will be determined which effects a risk occurrence would have, that is, which strategies and goals would be adversely affected. By the way, the referencing of objectives is omitted in some cases where the objective influence can be implicitly determined from the strategy-objective references.

4.2.4 Modeling an Enterprise Architecture

The previously described activities of the Horus method mainly intend to define the basis and framework of a business process analysis. The importance of these activities should not be underestimated, as they ensure that the executive management is effectively integrated into the project and the project costs remain within the planned budget. The subsequent modeling of the *enterprise architecture* shows, for the first time, the main features of the newly designed system. The description ensues from different angles, which is reflected in several interrelated submodels. Figure 4.10 shows the enterprise architecture modeling steps and model elements that are generated and processed.

4.2.4.1 Analysis of Business Process Architecture

The central model of the enterprise architecture is the *business process architecture model*. It is developed based on the context model and contains the most important business processes of the enterprise or of the system under consideration. In practice, such architecture models include two—in exceptional cases up to three—levels of modeling. It should always be ensured, however, that the model hierarchy

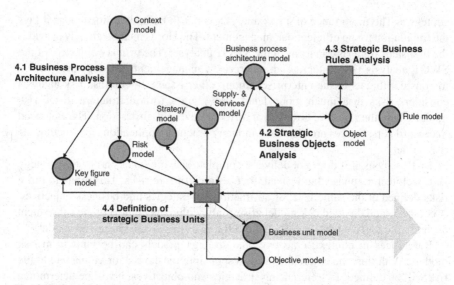

Fig. 4.10 Procedure model of enterprise architecture modeling (refinement of Step 4 from Phase 1)

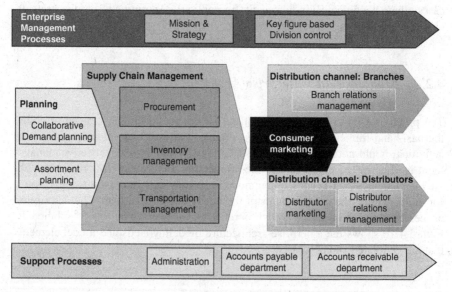

Fig. 4.11 Business process architecture model of the leather goods division

contains exactly one root to allow a complete view of the business process architecture at a glance—in practice often a demand difficult to fulfill.

Figure 4.11 models the view of the business process architecture of the leather goods division. For presentation purposes, an enhanced illustration is shown for which Horus provides a number of editing options.

In preparing the overview model, business processes are divided by corresponding graphical arrangement into three groups: *core processes*, *enterprise management processes*, and *support processes*. Core processes can be found in the center of Fig. 4.11; these are the ones where the actual enterprise value creation takes place. The planning, control and monitoring of core processes is carried out by the enterprise management processes, often placed in the upper region of the overview models. At the bottom, support processes create the enabling conditions for an efficient handling of core processes as well as enterprise management processes.

The leather goods division core business has been subdivided into processes that focus primarily on the business functions or the various distribution channels. This is quite typical for sales-oriented organizations. In contrast to this, product groups in development-intensive industries often form the primary criterion in the business process structure. Obviously, this has already taken place at a higher level in our example, as suggested by the name of the business division (leather goods).

In business process architecture models, the object flow relationships—as also seen in Fig. 4.11—are deliberately abstracted so as not to overload the models. However, this does not absolve the modeler from his task to not only identify the architecture model of the business processes, but also to show their mutual integration—a challenge to the modeler's graphic design expertise that is not to be underestimated. In refinements of the overview model, one often encounters the creative boundaries in practice and takes into account the object flow relations, which are important for an understanding in such cases.

Many references can be created from the business processes in the business process architecture model, since this model is indeed a central reference point for modeling. First, there is a connection to the system represented in the context model, as the business process architecture model, in fact, represents the refinement of this system. Using references into the strategy model, it is shown which strategies influence the specific business process. References to services in the supply and services model establish a link between the process and its value creation, therefore defining the process performance. Which key indicators will be used to measure the process outcome and by what risks it is affected, shall be determined with the referencing of key figures or risks.

4.2.4.2 Analysis of Strategic Business Objects

Especially when some highly integrated business software is to be used for the implementation of an enterprise architecture, business objects get a higher significance. As *master data*, they form the central focal point of the enterprise software solution. For this reason, the Horus method considers the creation of an *object model* already within the strategy and architecture phase. The business objects identified are associated with the business process architecture model through references, in order to show which processes (reading, writing, updating) access the objects in what ways.

The *strategic business object model* includes, in this early phase of modeling, only strategically important business objects (such as Order, Product, Customer with the specializations Consumer, and Distribution partner with the specializations Branch and Distributor), whereby the specification of attributes becomes largely unnecessary. Attributes that are important for the distinction of the different object types or are characteristic for the enterprise or industry form an exception.

As an example of a Horus object model, Fig. 4.12 shows a view of the leather goods division business objects relevant to sales and marketing. The multilevel specializations shown are typical, beginning, for example, with the marketing campaign or the customer and allowing for an object view at different levels of abstraction. An aggregation has been formed for the order that consists of an order header and either standard order positions or call positions of a connected basic agreement. The modeler's responsibility lies in whether objects have already been considered in the strategy and architecture phase that are more of an operational nature. As an example, this is the marketing campaign with their specializations Distributor acquisition and Consumer campaign.

The object model of the strategy and architecture phase is used as a starting point for a complete Object model in the subsequent business process analysis phase (see Sect. 4.3.1). The strategic business objects then become objects or aggregates (root objects with related objects). Further attributes and relationships are defined within the detailed object models and additional objects are introduced, which are

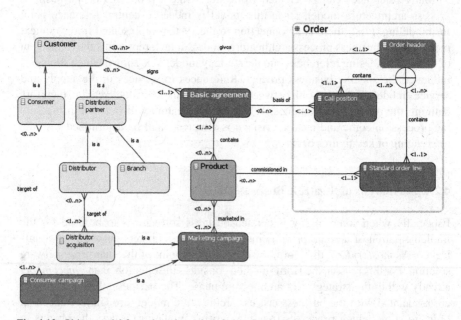

Fig. 4.12 Object model from the sales point of view for the leather goods division

necessary for the typification of object stores in the procedure models as well as the formulation of business rules.

4.2.4.3 Analysis of Strategic Business Rules

Each organization is aware of a set of *rules* that must be respected across the organization, that is, principally in all business processes. It is now possible to model these rules in all relevant processes explicitly. However, such an approach would preprogram inconsistencies between the various regulatory entities as well as high overhead for a change in the rules. For this reason, the Horus method provides that business rules are positioned and maintained in one central location—the *business rule model*.

The strategic business rule model, which is created in the strategy and architecture phase, includes only those rules that can be formulated by linking business processes and strategic business objects. Rules that relate to attributes and non-strategic properties should still be abstracted from at this point. A complete rule model will be created in the business process analysis phase (see Sect. 4.3.1 for an example of a Horus rule model).

References to the business process architecture model define which rule applies to which business process. References to the object model show the strategic business objects from which it is formulated.

4.2.4.4 Analysis of Strategic Business Units

In practice, the design of an organizational structure is at the center and often at the beginning of an organizational project. This means that such optimization potential will be wasted which results from an (inappropriate) alignment of the organizational structure to the business processes. It need not be mentioned that, especially, these are generally the most interesting potentials. To prevent such situations, the Horus method consciously goes without the modeling of a detailed organizational structure in the strategy and architecture phase. It is advisable, however, to introduce existing strategic business units that can then be used to define responsibilities. For the leather goods division, these could be units, for example, for branch operations, distributor business, and the area-wide management of the supply chain.

A complete organization structure is formed only at the end of the business process analysis phase and is then derived from the procedure models in conjunction with the other submodels (see Sect. 4.3.3 for an example of a Horus organization model in Fig. 4.22).

The large number of references that are established by the business units makes it clear that the business unit model also is a central reference point for modeling. In essence, the references are used to define *duties* and *responsibilities* of the business units. Specifically, the following references are then established: The link between business units and processes in the business process model defines which business processes fall into in the area of responsibility of the business unit. From references into the object model, it becomes clear which business unit is individually responsible for the existence, quality, and completeness of a given strategic business object. In addition, it can be specified which business unit is responsible for defining and maintaining a specific business rule. Responsibilities can be defined by references to strategies and objectives; however, it can also be shown which strategies and objectives influence the business unit.

The creation of value that a business unit adduces can be determined by references into the supply and services model. In this case, those benefits are referenced that are performed by the business unit. Indirect participation in the context of leadership or support processes is not included in the reference. However, internal services can be defined for such processes that can then also be referenced.

Finally, one can specify which key figures can be defined and monitored by a business unit. The referencing of risks defines for which risks the business unit will assume responsibility. Responsibility comprises the definition of the risk, appropriate risk prevention, and responses to the actual risk itself.

4.2.5   System Architecture Design

The architecture of the systems to support business processes is determined by the requirements that can be derived from the results of the business process analysis. However, such an ideal-typical approach is generally not practical, since the project principal would like to receive clarity concerning the expected level of investment at a very early stage. The Horus method therefore provides a broad *system architecture design* at the end of the strategy and architecture phase. This occurs at a very abstract level but allows for a first indication of the procurement and implementation costs, as well as anticipated operating costs.

Horus provides a *resource model* for system architecture design. It describes the expected target state of the architecture. The resource model focuses on components for building the system architecture, that is, primarily on hardware and network infrastructure as well as on the planned software components. Figure 4.13 shows an example of the system architecture model for the leather goods division. It describes an Oracle Applications environment that is divided into hardware, system software, and application software components. The subcomponents themselves can also again be disassembled, as shown in the example of the production environment. The system architecture is pretty concrete already, particularly concerning the application software. This is necessary, as the system architecture model provides the basis for budget as well as ROI calculations. One can work with empirical values regarding the hardware, so that a clarification in the sense of manufacturer names can be dispensed.

The system architecture design represents only one possible use of the resource model. Resource terms are broadly defined in the Horus method and include human

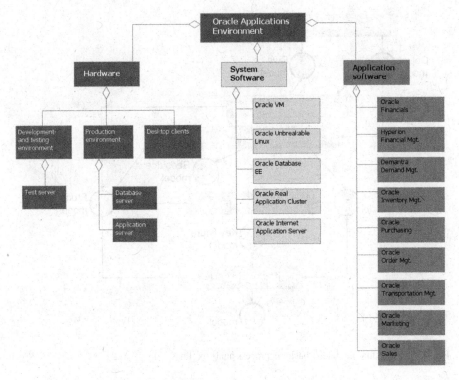

Fig. 4.13 System architecture model of the leather goods division

resources as well as machinery, equipment, real estate, or intangible assets (e.g., software licenses). In practice, resource models, both in the strategy and architecture phase and in the business process analysis phase (see Sect. 4.3.3), are always used when it comes to the consideration of the availability and costs of scarce resources.

References can be established from the resources of the system architecture model to define which resources (system components) are available to support the business process. Which resources will be used (system components) for processing business objects depends on the references into the object model. Finally, it will be determined which business units are responsible for the resource (system component).

4.3 Phase 2: Business Process Analysis

Business process analysis is carried out in Phase 2 of the Horus method within the frame that has been marked out as a result of the strategy and architecture phase. That framework defines both the width and depth of the analysis area, including in particular where the focus of the analysis lies. The models to be created in Phase 2

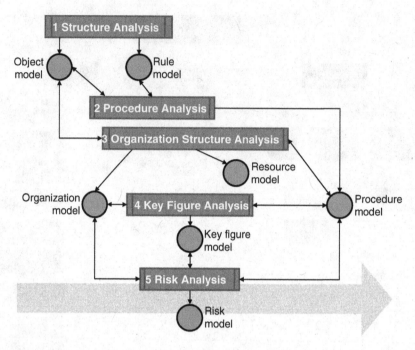

Fig. 4.14 Procedure model for business process analysis (Phase 2)

are in part further refinements of the Phase 1 models, displaying the facts in much greater detail and less of a strategic rather than a technical point of view.

Figure 4.14 shows the procedure model of the business process analysis phase, where the individual activities have been divided into five areas of responsibility. The activity refinements will be explained in detail in subsequent sections. It should be noted that for the activities during business process analysis causal dependencies are defined that allow for a concurrent execution of these activities. In practice, this always results in interesting potentials to shorten project times.

Structure analysis is the entry point into business process analysis, where the business objects as well as the business rules are defined that span the business process in question. On this basis, *procedure analysis* is carried out, for which two alternative analytical techniques have proven successful: *event analysis* as well as *use case analysis*. Subsequent tasks are the linking of the procedure model with the existing structural models and the progressive refinement of the activities. The details of the activities are modeled levelwise in a recursive manner.

Organization structure analysis includes the design of the organizational structure with the definition of roles and responsibilities. Key figures and risks will be subsequently defined based on the processes and the organization structure. Both the key figure analysis and risk analysis tasks, which are closely linked, are often processed in parallel.

4.3.0.1 Defining the Modeling Strategy

In larger projects, it is advisable to conduct a decomposition of the modeling tasks into manageable work packages. To this end, the overall system is broken down into segments, which are then processed individually. The resulting partial models are subsequently integrated into an overall model. The segmentation is carried out by linking individual processes to process clusters, which are then processed together. Ideal typical clusters are formed from processes that are linked together through numerous links and only a few—or ideally none—show connections outside of the cluster. Based on the resulting clusters, a strategy is formed to determine how the clusters will be executed. The parallelization of tasks, which is easily possible for ideal typical clusters, offers good starting points for a reduction of project time at the expense of potentially higher resource requirements.

4.3.1 Structure Analysis

In discussing the Horus method, the significance of the procedures in business process analysis is repeatedly emphasized. Therefore, it is perhaps surprising that a structural analysis is made at the initial stage of a business process analysis. Experience gained from practical applications has shown that it is important to create a cross-process generic structured framework of objects and business rules, then modeling the relevant processes in this context. This can certainly produce conceptual parallels to the object-oriented analysis. Figure 4.15 shows the steps of structure analysis and the model elements that are created and processed.

What are the advantages in following such a procedure? Primarily, experience shows that modelers tend to describe very many issues directly within procedure models. One works with "questionable" object stores and lengthy textual descriptions in order to specify cross-process valid structures that could be modeled more elegantly to avoid redundancy in objects and business rules. An initial structural analysis helps to avoid such modeling errors. In addition, it establishes a common

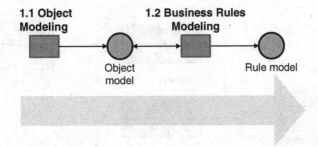

Fig. 4.15 Procedure model of structure analysis (refinement of Step 1 from Phase 2)

understanding of the technical contents of the business process analysis, thus facilitating a uniform and understandable concept formation in model building.

4.3.1.1   Object Modeling

Based on the business objects identified during strategy analysis, a more detailed *object model* will be created within the scope of the structural analysis. The term *object* (short for object type) is purposely used very broadly here. It refers to information and knowledge objects as well as to specific real-world objects (products, raw materials, and supplies, etc.) and, if necessary, to living beings. Objects are formally described through their attributes and their relationships to other objects. The Horus object model has a clearly defined semantics that allows for a bidirectional mapping between objects or aggregates on the one hand and XML objects on the other. In this respect, the object model can also be used for the graphical specification of XML structures.

The object model requires a certain sense of flair on the modeler's part; otherwise, there is the danger that modeling costs will explode. The primary goal is to create an object-oriented basis for the subsequent specification of processes and business rules. Attributes will be considered only insofar as required for the formulation of rules and regulations or to understand the object semantics. In particular, it must be clear that additional implementation-oriented objects and relationships as well as complete lists of attributes and constraints would have to be defined for a database design that must still be implemented.

Figure 4.16 shows an example of the modeling of the object Order. First, an aggregate is formed which sets the order in its role as the root object in relation to its positions. Aggregates allow objects to be combined into a complex business object that can be referenced to as a whole. Order line is also linked with Product by a relationship, and Order with Distribution partner. This makes it clear that not all orders in the leather goods division will be made directly by consumers, but indirectly through distribution partners. The object types each contain simple attributes and constraints (e.g., assessment of the Release tag).

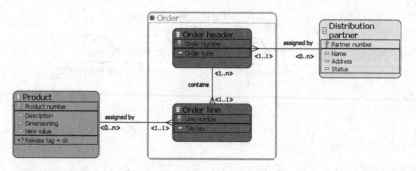

Fig. 4.16 Object model of object type Order

4.3.1.2 Modeling of Business Rules

Business rules are becoming immensely important, especially in a service-oriented architecture because they represent an elegant way to formulate a special form of semantic constraints that must be met by all services at all times. Even in business process analysis, they help to "purify" the procedures of general rules and keep models understandable. One can then simply imagine that the business rules are implicitly embedded in all transition rules of the procedure models. For the purposes of Petri net semantics (see Sect. 3.3), they represent additional preconditions for the implementation of activities, also being able to prevent these if they are violated. Business rules are used for different purposes, for example, to regulate access rights, to conduct general business calculations (e.g., calculation of cash flow or gross margin), or for the establishment of enterprise regulations. When a business rule violation occurs, an exceptional situation arises that must be dealt with, according to predefined procedures.

The Horus method intentionally limits itself to a very simple form of rule modeling. Rules are defined only in semiformal notation in conjunction with textual descriptions. A formal specification of the rules is only possible in a subsequent design phase according to the requirements and with the appropriate tools to implement the target system.

In the Horus method, business rules consist of *events*, *conditions*, and *actions* ("ECA"). The *event* defines the scope of the rule, in particular when the rule will be applied and in what professional context, that is, in which areas of the business model. *Conditions* are usually written in a pseudolanguage that allows a sufficiently precise specification, while at the same time not overstraining the department staff. Finally, *actions* are defined that are to be carried out in case of a breach of the business rule—also in a pseudolanguage. Actions include, in most cases, both automated activities (i.e., the release of warnings, initiation of workflows, or the launch of application or system programs) as well as manual activities (e.g., examination or correction processes).

Figure 4.17 shows an example of two business rules for the leather goods division. The first rule ensures that the enterprise will always offer competitive prices. The second rule ensures the integrity of the distributor data, by guaranteeing that only distributors with a good credit rating are kept and who are active in the market. The examples show, by using a pseudolanguage, how a semi-formal nature of the rule model can be achieved. A complete description of the language syntax is omitted here, as it goes beyond the scope of this book. As part of rule modeling, references to objects and aggregates are built into the object model, which document to which objects and relationships the rules are formulated in each case.

4.3.2 Procedure Analysis

Horus procedure models are distinguished by the fact that they are simple and still show a high expressive power. However, in practice, it repeatedly turns out that

Business rule: COMPETITIVE PRICING

Make sure that no competitor in the market offers cheaper products (price leadership) and that campaign prices are never higher than regular list prices.	
Definition:	
Event:	Current-market analysis has been done **OR** marketing campaign has been defined **OR** list prices have changed
Condition:	**EXISTS** product for which a competitor offers a better price **OR EXISTS** campaign price > list price
Action:	**ALERT** marketing management **AND START WORKFLOW** perform complete market analysis **AND CREATE REPORT** campaign prices

Business rule: DISTRIBUTOR INTEGRITY

Only those distributors with good credit rating and sufficient market activity are kept and supported.	
Definition:	
Event:	**BEGIN OF WEEK** /* weekly check */ **OR INSERT** distributor /* registration of a new distributor */
Condition:	**EXISTS** distributor with credit rating worse than B **OR EXISTS** distributor which (for at least one product line misses the agreed contract volume **AND** number of marketing campaigns per year < 2)
Action:	**ALERT** management of indirect sales **AND ALERT** account manager (distributor) **AND START WORKFLOW** violation of distributor integrity

Fig. 4.17 Business rules for the leather goods division

creating a model sets significantly higher demands to the structuring and abstraction abilities than the reading and understanding of the resulting model. Remedial action can only be taken with a systematic methodical approach, such as the Horus method offers. Horus offers two alternative approaches for this that can be combined. Figure 4.18 shows the steps of the procedure analysis and the model elements that are created and processed.

4.3.2.1   Procedure Analysis Using the Business Event Method

Processes are perceived in their environment, above all, in that they respond to business events and even create events themselves. Especially with event-intensive

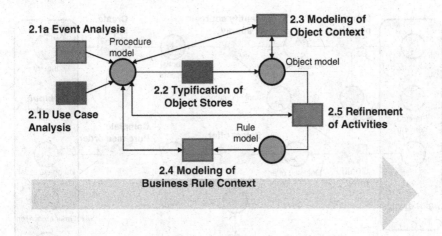

Fig. 4.18 Procedure model of procedure analysis (refinement of Step 2 from Phase 2)

processes, which are generally characterized by relatively short chains of activity, it has therefore been proven useful to precede procedure modeling with an *event analysis*. This happens only in the context of the procedure.

In event analysis, a distinction is made between output events that occur later in the procedure model as output object stores of the modeled network and input events, the input object stores. Event analysis is based on a retrograde approach, whereby modeling takes place from the output events in the direction of the input events. One starts with the output events and then considers what activities generate these events. Based on these activities, activity chains are modeled in the direction of the input events until a connection to those events is possible.

Figure 4.19 illustrates an example of an event analysis. Here, the inquiry is interpreted as an output event, and the requisition as well as the planned demands as input events. Based on the inquiry, the activity Create inquiry is found that leads to the object store Potential suppliers to Identify sources of supply and finally to Demand planning, which is triggered by requisitions and calculated planned demands.

4.3.2.2   Procedure Analysis Based on the Use Case Method

As an alternative to an event analysis, procedure analysis can be based on the *use case method*. This has the advantage that a modeler needs less abstraction skills. Use cases are collected and converted into simple model fragments. These fragments are then grouped according to technical criteria and are integrated into related procedure models. The integration usually takes place through shared object stores or activity chains.

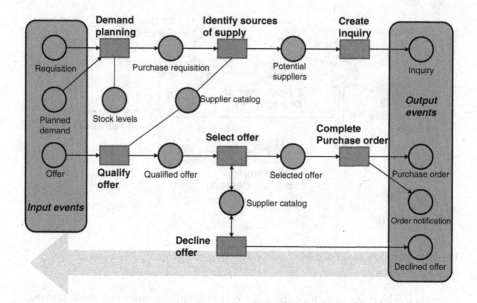

Fig. 4.19 Principle of event-oriented procedure analysis

Figure 4.20 shows the principle of the use case method. Separate use cases are modeled for the processing of requisitions or planned demands. Identifying supply sources can be used with the integration of these use cases, taking place in both cases based on the supplier catalog, subsequently determining the potential suppliers in each case. The integrated procedure model could then look like the one in Fig. 4.19. It is clear that the central integration structure is not always so obvious in practice as it is in this example. Identical situations often hide behind different designated activities and object stores.

4.3.2.3 Typing Object Stores and Modeling of Object Context

Further model details must be developed based on the results of a procedure analysis. First, a typing of the procedure model object stores is made. In some cases, existing objects and aggregates can be referenced for this purpose. In many cases, however, new objects or aggregates must also be defined and then referenced in the object store. By the way, a very important advantage of the aggregates is that even in the case of complex business objects only a single element, namely the aggregate of the Object model, must be referenced.

Finally, thought must be given to which central objects are still needed in order to formulate the activity rules (often, these are objects that are found in the target system as master data objects). These objects usually are accessed in read-only

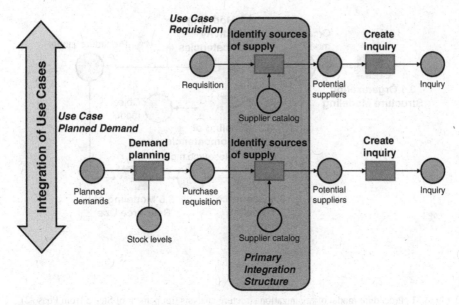

Fig. 4.20   Principle of use case-oriented procedure analysis

manner and have therefore not yet been used to model the causal dependencies between activities.

4.3.2.4   Modeling of Business Rule Context

Although modeling with business rules provides for significant advantages in simplifying the models, it does have one major drawback: It is not apparent at first glance what business rules are really relevant in the context of the respective activity. For this reason, it is possible to allocate those business rules directly to the activities that must be considered during their execution.

4.3.3   Organization Structure Analysis

At this point of business process analysis, the cross-process objects and business rules have been designated, and based on this, procedures have been defined. An organizational structure is derived next and is linked to the other model components through various references. Responsibilities and competencies are defined through these references. Figure 4.21 shows the steps of the *organization structure analysis* and the model elements that are created or processed.

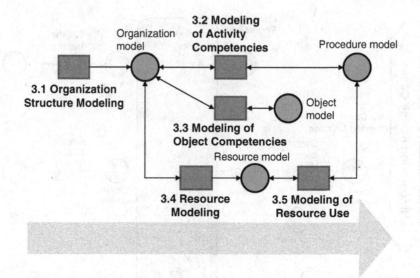

Fig. 4.21 Procedure model of organization structure analysis (refinement of Step 3 from Phase 2)

4.3.3.1 Modeling the Organizational Structure

When modeling the organizational structure, the business unit structure from the strategy and architecture phase forms a superordinate framework that will now be filled with organization units. The organization units are arranged in a hierarchical structure, whereby cross-connections between subtrees of the hierarchy and distinctions between disciplinary and professional associations, or between line and staff functions, become possible.

In the organization model shown in Fig. 4.22, this has been applied to the accounts receivable department, which is associated with the branch businesses in a disciplinary manner, but which exhibits an additional reporting line (discernible by the dotted edge) to distributor business. Division assistance is a typical example of a staff function.

The intended purpose of the model is crucial concerning the appropriate level of detail required of the organization model. A detailing up to the level of organization units for exclusive use in a business process analysis may be sufficient. It is necessary, however, to refine the organizational structure for personnel requirements planning or a subsequent workflow-based process implementation. In these cases, the staff required in the execution of the business processes must be explicitly considered. The Horus method provides a dual approach for this purpose. Firstly, palpably available staff members can be assigned to the organization units. In addition, a percentage distribution of availability is possible over several organization units. This concept is only suitable for documentation purposes, however, and labor law problems must be pointed out here, even when simulation and analysis is carried out.

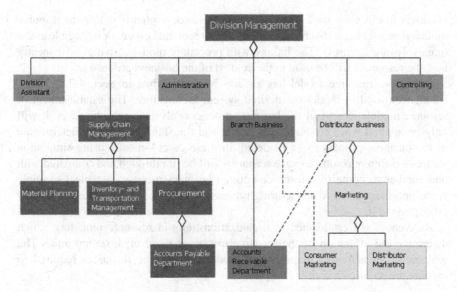

Fig. 4.22 Organization model of the leather goods division

Horus therefore supports a *role concept*. The organization units are assigned roles from which the referencing from the procedure models then ensues. The models will then become independent of staff turnover. More importantly, however, the commercial practice, in which the staff plays different roles, must allow itself to be comfortably modeled. This also applies to representation provisions. As required, the model roles can also be assigned to specific employees.

4.3.3.2 Referencing the Organizational Structure

Horus offers extensive options for defining details of organization units and their relationships. A high significance is also put on the references that are established between the organization units and other parts of the business process model. References are established to objects and activities within the process models. In which order this occurs is left up to the modeler's discretion. Activity references define which role is required in which organization unit for the implementation or is responsible for it. The organization unit that is responsible for existence, quality, and integrity of the object and/or the aggregate that is responsible defines the referencing of objects or aggregates.

4.3.3.3 Resource Modeling

As described above, the Horus method considers the required personnel in the implementation of the required business processes in terms of roles and staff that are assigned to organization units. Staff may also be interpreted as a special type of *resource*. In this case, staff resources could be stored explicitly within the resource model. Resources can also be machinery, equipment, real estate, or intangible assets (e.g., software licenses). The linking with procedure model activities will specify how the resources will be used in the context of the business processes.

A generic resource model has already been described in Sect. 4.2.5. There, it has been used to model the desired system architecture. The establishment of resource models as part of the business process analysis is rare, however. It will only be applied when resources are scarce and the shortage is a key determinant of the business process to be modeled. In these cases—mostly using simulation studies—different resource usage scenarios will be run through and compared with one another to come to a resource-optimal business process. A typical example is the optimization of manufacturing processes that make mutual use of a narrow production unit.

References are established to organization units in resource modeling which determine the affiliation of the resource to one or more organization units. The referencing of activities in procedure models defines the resources required to execute the required activity.

4.3.4   Key Figure Analysis

Organizations that focus firmly on their business processes are ideally suited for key-figure-based management systems. With regard to the remarks concerning the Balanced Scorecard in Sect. 4.1.3, it is essential to measure company performance based on not only (historical) financial results but along the entire supply chain. These include systems that are made up of key indicators that span the supply chain. Figure 4.23 shows the steps of a key figure analysis and the model elements that are created or processed.

4.3.4.1   Procedure-Oriented Key Figure Analysis

As part of the Horus method, the measuring along the entire supply chain can be achieved by looking along the procedure models for suitable measuring points, depicting these as corresponding key figures. For each key figure, it will be defined how, at which times, and in which intervals it will be measured. For this, minimum and maximum values, tolerances and thresholds are given. The perspectives of the Balanced Scorecard have once again proven itself for key figure structuring.

4.3.4.2   Organization-Based Key Figure Analysis

An alternative to the analysis of appropriate key figures is an approach that forms key figures based on organizational structure. Although this approach is more

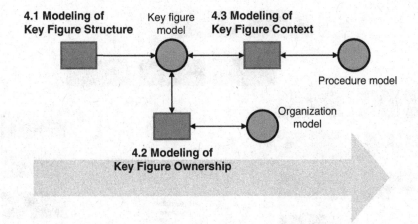

Fig. 4.23 Procedure model of key-figure analysis (refinement of Step 4 from Phase 2)

popular in practice, the validity and performance of the emerging key figure systems is significantly less than that in a procedure-oriented approach. This is because it is as easily possible to uncover mistakes, yet a root cause analysis is much more difficult without an allocation to the processes responsible for this.

Figure 4.24 shows an example of a key figure system for the leather goods division. The key figure model depicted is structured in accordance with the perspectives of the Balanced Scorecard mentioned above, as frequently encountered in practice. There are also other common structuring criteria, such as structuring according to various business units, product lines, responsibilities, or a combination of different criteria. In the context of comprehensive key figure systems, generalizations or specializations are to be found in any case that create a hierarchical order within key figure branches. The example shows this for profitability, which represents a generalization of sales profitability, return on assets, and return on investment (ROI). The quality is modeled as a generalization, since it is measured over four different key figures. The return rate remains interesting, which also represents a specialization of quality and service capability.

In addition to typical quantitative key figures (such as the ROI), the key figure model regularly contains qualitative key figures based on an assessment by responsible persons or experts. In some cases, rather "dubious" quantitative variables are combined with qualitative assessments. This may hold true, for example, for the key figure university contacts, since the number of contacts alone says little about their true benefit.

Key figures are linked by references to organization units. The "owner" of a key figure is defined in this way. He or she is responsible for the key figure specification and its monitoring. References to activities in procedure models document, in context of which activities the key figure is relevant.

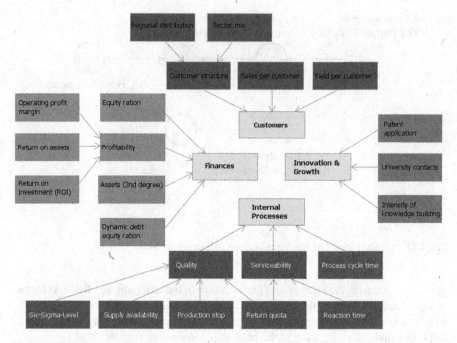

Fig. 4.24 Key figure model of the leather goods division

4.3.5   Risk Analysis

Risk analysis strongly resembles key figure analysis in its approach. One correspondingly distinguishes between a procedure-oriented and an organization-based risk analysis here. Figure 4.25 shows the steps of a risk analysis and the model elements that are created and processed.

4.3.5.1   Procedure-Oriented Risk Analysis

Procedure-oriented risk analysis is mainly used when the risks are to be determined along a core business process. In such cases, risks are identified along the procedure models and are specified by the probability of occurrence and the anticipated risks. In practice, procedure-oriented risk analysis is usually associated with a procedure-oriented key figure analysis, because a directly related key figure is defined for the risks found to ensure an immediate response to the risk occurrence.

4.3.5.2   Organization-Based Risk Analysis

In practice, organization-based risk analysis is more common. It has the advantage that the risk responsibilities can be derived directly from the model. Instead of an

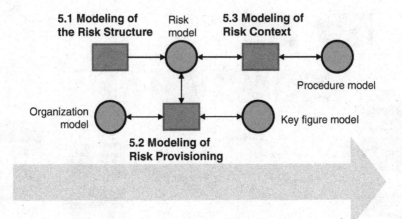

Fig. 4.25 Procedure model of risk analysis (refinement of Step 5 from Phase 2)

accountability concept, it is often spoken of *ownership*, to express full responsibility for the risk definition associated with its monitoring and the response to the risk. Key figures are sought after in the organization-based risk analysis to monitor the risks, which in many cases originate from different parts of the supply chain.

Figure 4.26 shows an example of a risk model for the leather goods division. Although not essential, this risk model has again been structured according to the perspectives of the Balanced Scorecard. This is also good practice as well as the abbreviated designation of risks. For example, the risk of lacking manufacturing capacities is referred to only as Production capacity. In an accompanying textual description, the risk must then be explained and it must be shown, which steps have been taken to prevent the occurrence or to enable the early detection of the risk. The assignment of key figures to risks is important here. This formally describes which key figures serve to identify the danger of the materialization of risks at an early stage, possibly avoiding risks altogether, or at least as early as possible to initiate countermeasures.

For a better overview, risks are typically bundled in the form of generalizations, as is the case, for example, with compliance risks that encompass the Sarbanes-Oxley (SOX) and Good Manufacturing Practice (GMP) risks as well as risks arising from the breach of the Generally Accepted Accounting Principles (GAAP). It is also interesting that GAAP risks are equally assigned to the financial area by way of further generalization.

In the risk model, both internal and external risks are considered, such as the risk of stagnating target markets. In the example of innovation risks, it is shown how the internal risk of missing innovations is combined with the external risk of state obstacles to innovation.

Risks are linked by references to organization units. The risk "owner" is defined in this way. He is responsible for risk specification, risk management, and risk

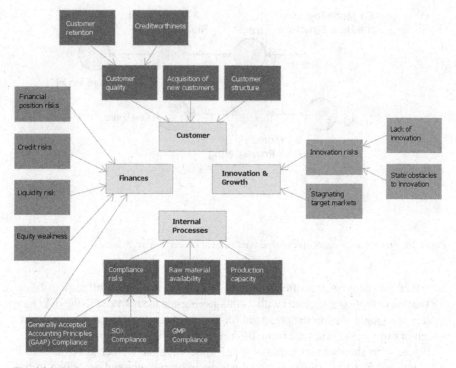

Fig. 4.26 Risk model of the leather goods division

monitoring. In this context, referencing of key figures is relevant which are used to monitor the risk. The Horus method summarizes the definition of ownership and the key figures under the term risk prevention. References to activities in procedure models document the risk relevance in the context of activities.

4.4 Simulation

The Horus method describes a consistent process for the comprehensive modeling of business processes within the framework of business process engineering. The central point of reference is represented by XML nets that offer, by virtue of their operational semantics (see Chap. 3), formally sound opportunities for process *simulation*. A look at the business practice in connection with the simulation shows, however, a surprising ambivalence: Although the need for simulation is undisputed and every decision maker "lusts" for ways to test the consequences of his decision alternatives in advance, the simulation is often rejected based on the expected expenses for the preparation and execution of simulation studies. The added benefit generated by the simulation is considered to be too low, and simulation is often labeled as a cost driver.

This is different with the Horus method: It comprehends simulation as a key to significantly increasing the benefits arising from business process engineering. The use of simulation-capable models in the Horus method provides for a substantial reduction in simulation efforts. Moreover, the seamless integration of modeling and simulation—which is also reflected in the Horus tools—enables entirely new forms of project communication, which are reflected directly in the quality of project work and the results achieved.

In the following section, the cyclic procedure in the simulation will be described first. On that basis, it is shown in Sect. 4.4.2 how the simulation is embedded within the Horus method.

4.4.1 The Simulation Cycle

In the Horus method, simulation is based on the simulation of XML nets as described in Chap. 3 (and more formally defined in literature). This is extended here to parameterize the models (see Sect. 4.4.3) and is then embedded in a methodical manner. Simulation is an inherently iterative process. In this respect, it does not suffice to introduce a "simulation" method step; in fact, simulation must be regarded as a cyclic process, which is then specifically introduced into the methodical procedure.

Figure 4.27 shows a simulation cycle consisting of six steps. The starting point is to define the *simulation goals* in line with the *simulation strategy* chosen. This first step is of crucial importance, because the course will be set here for the costs that will incur because of the simulation. Therefore, in practice, it usually does not make sense to model all business processes with all their contexts and then apply a simulation after that. What should be proven or shown with this overall simulation? In addition, what lessons can be learned from which simulation results? Questions of this nature must be asked before making an investment in simulation. Benefit-oriented, considerations then quickly lead to a limitation of simulation space for such procedures, which require a detailed analysis due to their complexity, their potential for change or their dependency on external influences. Alternatively, statements must be made concerning the behavior of the "under load" procedure. The three big questions will then be summarized in this first step of the simulation cycle: What is being simulated, why, and how?

Several alternative solutions are usually compared as part of a simulation. To that extent, various *model variants* will be appropriated for the simulation relevant area, which are then evaluated and compared through simulation. Model variants often differ only in their parameters (see Sect. 4.4.3); in other cases, structurally different model variants will be compared to one another. Step 3 includes the above-mentioned *parameterization*, that is, the extended attributes of model elements that go beyond the XML net notation introduced in Chap. 3. The XML net simulation offers, to some extent, the "carrier semantics" for the execution of the broader Horus business process models. Step 4 then includes the actual *simulation* of the

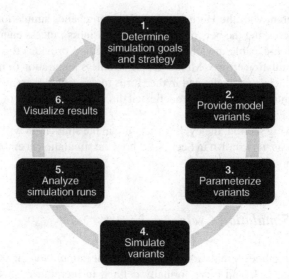

Fig. 4.27 The simulation cycle

model variants, which takes place in the form of an interpretation and execution of the models. As a result, runtime data of the simulation arises that is *analyzed* and compared with each other or against benchmarks in Step 5 (see also Sect. 4.4.5). In conclusion, the simulation results will then be visualized. *Visualization* here denotes the graphical animation of the processes and the overall analysis results in the form of graphs and tabular reports.

At this point, it should be noted that the simulation cycle described is often not consistently run sequentially in practice. It sees itself more as a basic principle, which presents itself through the multiple overlapping of steps in practice and a quite deliberate testing of process ideas.

4.4.2   Application Areas

In practice, simulation is used in all phases of business process engineering as well as in cross-project tasks. Simulation is a powerful tool for the project manager and quality assurer for various planning, control, and monitoring tasks. However, the goals and strategies associated with the simulation will differ severely in the phases, as the following statements will explain.

4.4.2.1   Phase 1: Strategy and Architecture

The models created in Phase 1 of business process engineering are still hardly formalized. What meaning might a simulation have that plays out its advantages especially when different formal aspects directly interlock within the models? In fact, the simulation does not come close to a quality assurance role or even the final proof of benefits of an overall solution. Rather, in this phase, simulation assumes the character of an exploratory prototyping: In actual-state procedures, vulnerabilities are identified and the consequences resulting therefrom are disclosed. Conversely, strengths will be identified in connection with possibilities to systematically develop these further. The primary goal is to provide a platform through simulation, allowing an objective assessment of actual-state processes, additionally promoting process innovation or at least new ideas, making the assessment of its feasibility possible.

The simulation models created in Phase 1 mostly possess a "throwaway character," that is, they will not become part of the final business process specification. Nevertheless, it is recommended that exploration models are deposited into the repository together with their analysis results to keep the decision-making process, that eventually led to the solutions adopted, comprehensible.

4.4.2.2 Phase 2: Business Process Analysis

As part of the business process analysis, an integration between modeling and simulation takes place that is more advanced than in Phase 1. Simulation now takes on a much more iterative, evolutionary nature, that is, the simulation models developed progressively come closer to the final project results achieved during the course of the analysis. In this respect, the simulated models, in connection with their analysis results, will become integral components of the final business process specification.

Simulation generally assumes a quality-assurance purpose in business process analysis, that is, the validity of a solution is proven through simulation, whereby the evidence takes place both analytically and visually by procedure animation—through the application of Petri net firing rules and the evaluation of key indicators. Simulation provides a valuable service in organizational *change management* as well, when it comes to convincing management or the business user of the benefits of a chosen solution.

Simulation is indispensable when it comes to "under load" testing of processes and comparing different variants in terms of their performance with each other. Not infrequently, process variations assert themselves as a result of simulation examinations, which are suboptimal at low load—that is, at low occupancy of the object stores—however cope with large loads much better than competing process variations. Typical application fields for simulation are also the processes that underlie very strong external influences, which can be most difficult to plan in advance—these are often found in the form of external entities within the model. Examples are applications in the business-to-consumer (B2C) area, which must respond to significant load fluctuations.

Just one word about *process optimization*, which is often associated with simulation in a direct relationship. To be very clear: Simulation is not an optimization technique! Rather, it is an important tool for optimization by examining alternative solutions and comparing these, thus providing valuable information for process improvement. The benefits of simulation in finding solution ideas cannot be overstated—however, it cannot compensate for human creativity.

4.4.2.3   Phase 3: Usage

The simulation application does not end with the existence of a completed business process specification but extends into the entire life cycle of the process, well into the use phase. In business process management and during process implementation, business change management forms an important field of application. Simulation helps to convince decision makers and users of the viability of a solution. A professional reaction to changes of the economic and organizational process environment is possible with simulation studies by showing effects of changes in terms of opportunities and risks transparently, and with a sound quantitative basis. In many cases, simulation results are also the starting point for improving the current processes or perhaps for a complete business process reengineering.

One application field that is becoming increasingly important, given the uncertain and difficult to forecast economic trends, is *advance planning of corporate key figures* (predictive planning). Conventional planning methods are based on past observations, enriched with strategic objectives and market forecasts, which in turn are based on historical data and are continued into the future. Given the increasingly frequent global crises—whether in business, in the environment, or in politics—and the resulting changes, these procedures no longer allow reliable forecasts. What is needed is not planning but a series of different planning scenarios, each of which is based on different assumptions concerning the relevant enterprise environment. Predictive planning offers an ideal field of activity for simulation, in which different environmental conditions can be run through with simulation, where planning can then be optimized in this regard.

4.4.3   Creation and Parameterization of Model Variants

So far, the simulation of the business process model created has been discussed in simplified terms and the fact that it is based on the XML net transition rule described in Chap. 3. These statements will be refined in this section to better assess not only the possibilities but also the limitations of simulation. In the previous section, it was explained that in a simulation, not only the business process model is often simulated, but also several variants of this model are compared against each other using the simulation results. These variants often differ only in their parameterization; sometimes it also involves structurally different models. The management of the model variants is a task that can be achieved quite efficiently with the help of database-based repositories, as offered by Horus.

For the evaluation of the simulation possibilities, it is important to know that not all components of a Horus business process model will be considered in a

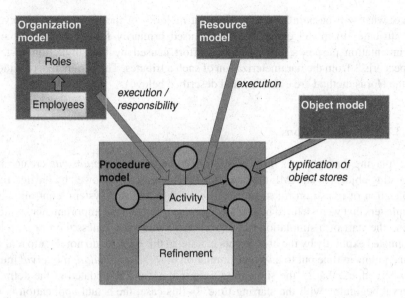

Fig. 4.28 Simulation relevant components of a business process model

simulation. Relevant are only those model components that have a direct formal connection to XML nets, which form the central reference point in the simulation model. Figure 4.28 clearly emphasizes this connection. In addition to the XML-net-based procedure model, the resource model is relevant, as well as the roles in the organization model. Behind the roles are employees who assume the execution of the activities or are responsible for them. Resources are physical resources or even human resources, necessary for the implementation of the activities. Lack of personnel or resource capacities can lead to activities not being executed, even though the XML net transition rule would allow this. This fact is "played with" during simulation: Model variants are produced by capacity variations, or simulation runs are played through without capacity limitations to determine what maximum capacity would be required for trouble-free operation.

Relevant for the simulation is also the object model that provides the basis for the classification of the object stores in the procedure model, that is, the structure of the "flowing" objects in the procedure model results from the definition of the object model. Note that object models that are created in the strategy and architecture phase and include only strategic business objects are not of interest in a simulation because they have no formal correlation in connection with XML nets.

As mentioned above, the parameterization of model variants is of considerable importance, as for one thing the parameters potentially affect (more precisely: limit) the switching behavior and for another create the condition to determine important key figures such as cost, time, error rates, or value creation through simulation. Some of the simulation parameters are only there to control the simulation, in other words, to determine when it starts, in which intervals the simulation will take place, what will be animated, etc. The vast majority of the parameters, however, are attributes to model elements that are used primarily for static analysis and documentation purposes. No additional effort caused by the simulation in this respect arises from the parameterization of such attributes. The parameters provided by the Horus method are classified and described below.

4.4.3.1   Simulation Runs

The "playing through" of a procedure is referred to as a *simulation run*, created by allocating objects to an XML net or an XML net hierarchy, followed by the iterative application of transition rules. In this respect, it is a closed system, controlled by parameters that were defined beforehand. *Time parameters* are important here which define the start of a simulation run as well as an endpoint, unless the run is to be terminated explicitly by the user. Points in time, in this context, do not refer to real or actual points in time but to a virtual simulation of these. A *simulation interval* must also be defined, that is, the simulation time will always be updated in the defined interval beginning with the starting time. In this case, the actual application is to be kept in mind: For business processes, days or hours are likely to be useful and sometimes months or even years; for technical processes and embedded systems, however, minute, second, or millisecond intervals need to be applied.

A simulation run is always referring to a particular procedure model hierarchy. The latter results from a given procedure model which forms the top of the hierarchy as well as the desired hierarchy depth, that is, assumed as infinite by default. An abstraction from model details during simulation is possible by limiting the depth of hierarchy, in order to deliberately reduce the complexity of the simulation. The significance of the results must then be evaluated against the background of abstraction.

Capacities can be assigned to specific model elements in the business process model: to the object stores, the roles, and the resources. Testing the model under load during the simulation is then performed with respect to such capacity constraints. These restrictions are strictly defined and unchangeable in some cases. In other cases, however, the required capacities should be estimated and planned during the simulation. Good simulation practice is to first "run through" the model without consideration of capacity constraints in order to determine the actual capacities required. Comparative simulations under effective and full load quickly provide reliable evidence for an optimal choice of capacities.

The purpose of simulation also lies in the visualization of the planned processes, in addition to the extraction of quantitative results. For this purpose, an *animation* of the simulation runs will be offered. This is based on the results of the formal simulation, being adapted to the needs of the visualization through various animation parameters. It will be determined which procedure models from the simulated model hierarchy will be shown on the screen in the context of the animation. In addition, an animation speed will be defined, largely derived from the model complexity: The more complex the models, the slower the animation, so as not to overwhelm the viewer.

Finally, it will be determined whether actions are to take place as part of the animation that are defined at the activity level. From a technical point of view, actions can be implemented as program calls or Web services that are used to clearly define abstract operations for the user to understand. In practice, actions are executed by, for example, SAP routines or Web Services; sample reporting and analysis are presented; or explanatory video, image, and audio files will be used.

4.4.3.2 Activities

Activities as the active elements of an XML net are of special importance during a simulation. They carry a variety of simulation parameters, justifying the numerous applications of simulation. One important area is *activity-based costing* (see Sect. 4.4.4), for which simulation provides the necessary numerical data. To this end, *costs* are determined which arise during the implementation of each activity. These costs are shown with a minimum, maximum, and average value to reflect the expected fluctuation margin. In carrying out an activity, transportation costs usually also arise besides actual processing costs. These types of costs include both transport costs to the place of processing, within the scope of the processing (repositioning), and the removal for further processing or to the warehouse. In reality, it is common practice that special activities are introduced for costlier transits, which then only cause transportation costs and no processing costs. Alternatively, loading and unloading costs will be assigned as processing costs of the transportation activity in such cases.

It is interesting to contrast activity costs with the expected *value creation*. Value creation will also be defined with a minimum, maximum, and average value. Surprisingly, in this case, values less than 0 are possible. This allows activities to be defined whose implementation will lead to a negative value contribution. In practice, you will find such situations, for example, in connection with country-specific legal requirements that make postprocessing of products necessary, which, in global terms, incurs a negative created value.

In addition to value-based considerations, simulation in particular aims at an extraction of time and capacity-related statements. In this respect, the activities carry time parameters: *Processing time* defines the minimum, maximum, or average time required to process an activity. The accuracy of the time designation is selected depending on the specific application. *Transportation times* define the duration of conveyance to the place of processing in the context of the processing (repositioning) and the removal for further processing or to the warehouse. *Personnel and resource requirements* can be defined as capacity parameters. By designating personnel requirements, one can define how many employees are required for a specific role in the activity. Interestingly, 0 can be specified in order to easily define variants, which is then specifically abstracted from employee availability. Resource requirements will determine how large the number of required resources is in the context of the activity.

The transition rule for XML nets starts out from a simple time model in which the business facts relevant for time and capacity considerations can be depicted only with some difficulty. The Horus method has therefore extended this time model in a practice-oriented manner, which is reflected in a number of execution parameters that are defined at activity level. These parameters do not change the transition rule or even expand the number of possible transition operations; instead, the number of possible transition operations would be limited. This occurs first through a selection of the weekdays allowable for activity execution. An execution interval, which is used for all selected days, defines the time interval in the form of a start and end time within which the activity can be executed. This also means that the implementation of the activity must "fit" completely within the time interval. If an interruption of the implementation is to be made possible, then an additional parameter for this must be used. The execution parameters of the activity described here are already sufficient for many practical applications, so if, for example, only one work week (Monday to Friday) is to be established in conjunction with standard working hours (8:00 am to 5:00 pm). We refer to the possibilities that the parameters for roles and resources provide for analysis that is more detailed.

It is interesting to link time and capacity-related simulation results with statements regarding the quality of the process results. For this purpose, the activities can each have a *quality ratio* as well as an *error rate* assigned to them. The quality ratio specified is defined as a percentage of what effect the implementation of the activity will have on the generated objects. The quality may deteriorate within the activity (<0%), remain the same (0%), or even improve (>0%). The error ratio defines the error rate produced in the execution of the activity.

The parameters that have so far been mentioned for activities and that were described with the simulation-relevant semantics extend the standard capabilities of XML nets, with the goal to conveniently map business situations within the model. The Horus method also provides parameters that serve exclusively to control the simulation. The ability to define actions at activity level and their use in the scope of the animation has already been described above. Furthermore, so-called process time parameters can be used, which control the time interval in which the activity may be carried out in the simulation run. Times are respectively defined with the date and time. Timewise, the activity may then not be run before the earliest start time and not after the latest start time is reached. The final execution must be completed no later than the latest end time.

Of great practical relevance is the question of what happens when an activity is enabled multiple times at a given time, that is, the transition rule is fulfilled for different markings. Whether multiple executions of the activity are needed or not will be determined by a corresponding parameter. Moreover, what happens in cases where an activity cannot be completed due to the temporal availability of resources or roles, for example, on one working day and outstanding work must be completed the next day? Whether this is permitted or not can be controlled with the interrupt parameter.

A special activity is referred to as a *load generator*, which has no direct business equivalence. Its sole purpose is to generate objects that can then be processed within the simulation framework. Load generators offer the opportunity to produce objects "artificially" according to specific rules or alternatively access real data and use these in the simulation as objects with optimal realism. For this purpose, load generators can access files (typically Excel files) or input data from databases, files or via the Web using Web services. Web services are also used to create objects using statistical distribution functions. Normal, equal, Poisson, and exponential distributions are frequently used.

4.4.3.3 Object Stores

The Horus method provides for simulation-related parameters for the passive elements of XML nets as well. For a business understanding of these parameters, it has proven useful to visualize object stores as a warehouse. In connection with the movement of goods that take place in this warehouse, capacities, abstraction strategies, or costs must also be taken into consideration. Nevertheless, the parameters find application to all types of object stores, for document or data stores, for example.

The maximum number of objects to be stored in the object store is determined by the *capacity parameter*. Of course, it is also possible to work with a capacity of 1. Since distinguishable objects are used in the XML net, which individual object is taken from object store is relevant to the transition behavior. The Horus method assumes a FIFO strategy (first in, first out) as a default, where invariably the oldest possible object is removed. The user can select an alternative removal strategy by using a related parameter: LIFO (last in, first out), HIFO (highest in, first out), and LOFO (lowest in, first out). Sequence data (first, last) refer here to the time stamp of the stored objects, while height specifications (highest, lowest) reference the cost of the objects.

Variable storage costs need to be taken into account for a cause-related distribution of costs within the scope of activity-based costing. For this purpose, it can be defined at object store level which variable storage costs will arise at least, up to a maximum or on average per unit of time and object. The object store parameters are completed with *quality change*, which describes with which percentage rate the quality of a stored object changes per time unit, thus allowing conclusions regarding the actual useful life of the object. Deterioration of quality is specified by negative percentages, improvements (e.g., through maturing) with positive percentages.

4.4.3.4 Connections

Connections between activities and object stores can also be strengthened in their business management validity by a suitable parameterization. Let us first turn to the case where there is a conflict when applying a transition rule with respect to two or more connections. Conflicts are resolved by default in which all competing connections are interpreted as equiprobable. This approach often reflects the actual economic situation inadequately. For this reason, the Horus method provides a probability for connections by which conflicts are then resolved. Connections which will not be used for the synchronization always carry a probability of 0%. The sum of probabilities of competing connections must not necessarily yield 100%, because the probabilities are "normalized" at the time of the simulation.

In considering the item cost parameter, it becomes clear that a parameter which appears insignificant at first glance can indeed be of high business management relevance in the context of the simulation. Moreover, it is clear that a clean analytical consideration of the accompanying facts is hardly possible without tool support. The significance of the parameter depends on the type of connection as follows:

- *Reading*: The costs of the object read are interpreted as a kind of user fee that is charged a percentage of the reading activity as indicated.
- *Input*: For input connections, the object-cost percentage is always 100% because the object is consumed by the associated activity, and therefore, all costs are to be charged to this particular activity.
- *Output*: The object cost parameters of an output connection define what proportion of the total cost of the activity (see the comments on activities above) will be passed on through this connection. In this respect, the sum of percentages of all output connections of an activity must always amount to 100%.

Incidentally, the object cost parameters are not only used for cost distribution but also analogously for the distribution of value creation and materials costs. On the other hand, there is a separate parameter for the distribution of object times that determines which part of the object times are to be passed on upon activation. In contrast to the object cost parameters, the object times of the connections are independent of an activity and, therefore, added up must not yield 100%, as the following description shows:

- *Reading*: In the case of objects that are read, object times are not taken over so as not to artificially drive up the processing times for objects that are to be determined later.
- *Input*: With input connections, the parameter determines which part of the processing times burdening the consumed object is passed on in the context of the activity. Theoretically, a specification of 100% stands to reason, but this is not always practical. One thinks of supplies and materials, which very well carry processing and storage times, however, should not be added to the object times of the end product.
- *Output*: The object-time parameters of an output connection define which part of the time, which has been passed on to the output object, will actually be added. In the case of objects that do not result from the processing of previous objects in an activity, but are actually created in this activity, the parameter must be set to 0%. Zero percent then means that only the processing time of the activity to be created will be added the output object.

4.4.3.5 Roles

Role parameters are especially important if, within the scope of the simulation, personnel requirements or personnel costs are identified—for example, in activity-based costing—and are to be distributed as caused. A billing rate per unit is defined on a role level for cost accounting, from which the costs are to be determined resulting from the execution of the assigned activity. For simplicity, we abstract from the possibly varying cost rates of the employees who fulfill the role. Statements about the quality that is expected of an employee from the respective role in the execution of the referenced activity will be made with a quality indicator.

The temporal availability is defined at the employee level for capacity-related simulations. This takes place in the form of availability profiles in which standard and day-specific work hours are defined, as well as periods of nonavailability due, for example, to vacation, training, illness, or termination. At role level, the intensity of cooperation is defined, which allows conclusions about the specific time commitment to fill the role. With this, the practical requirement is taken into account that an employee might perform multiple tasks simultaneously in one period, thus simultaneously filling multiple roles.

4.4.3.6 Resources

Resources have similar parameters just as roles do. However, while roles only relate to the available personnel, the concept of the resource is much more generally applicable. In this respect, it may well be useful to consider personnel resources not through roles but as resources in the simulation, especially if the interaction with other types of resources (e.g., machinery) is relevant. Regarding availability, intensities and availability profiles are used as with the roles. With it, maintenance and repair windows or also technical restrictions can be portrayed regarding the simultaneous processing of work orders.

A defined resource can have several instances. Explicitly specifying the number of required resources obviates the need to define similar resources numerous times, especially low-cost ones (often low-value economic goods). Although one would suspect that integer values would make sense for the definition, real numbers will be used instead, in order to take into account the fact that physical resources may be allocated to different logical resources. Examples include the distribution of staff to different roles or the distribution of the availability of a machine to multiple machine groups.

A billing rate per unit is defined at resource level for cost accounting from which the costs are to be determined resulting from the execution of the assigned activity. Minimum, maximum, and average values are used to also portray the external reference of resources that can lead to cost fluctuations. Preproduction costs are considered in addition to the actual resource costs, which are charged per execution of an activity as minimum, maximum, or on average. Setup times will be defined analogously. The modeling of setup costs and times is only useful when objects are processed in lots.

The quality indicator defined at resource level allows a quality estimate that is expected of the resource in the execution of the referenced activity. In addition, an error rate can be specified stating what percentages of the resource-generated objects are likely to be flawed.

4.4.4   Simulation with Added Value, Costs, Time, and Quality

A quite considerable added value, which goes far beyond the known use of process simulations, can be created in the context of the simulation with the described simulation parameters. Benefit aspects that already arise from the simulation of the XML nets described in Chap. 3 will not be considered in this method chapter. It is clear that these aspects must be integrated into an overall consideration.

The added benefit of a simulation based on the Horus method primarily results from a comprehensive analysis of business performance indicators such as added value, cost, time, and quality. They are used not only for simulation but also primarily for documentation and are already in use for static analysis of business process models. Static analysis makes interesting "low-cost statements" possible, concerning the mentioned business management parameters, which will already satisfy many users of the Horus method. Static analysis, however, poses the disadvantage that it is restricted to local views of the overall process. In particular, it does not include the "individual history" of the objects processed in the model. One might object that activity and object costs may easily be added up over an entire procedure model hierarchy, thereby enabling a global overview of the process. One then neglects, however, that the finished objects have not been processed in all activities and stored in all object stores but have taken their individual way through the business process model.

Does a static consideration against this background then at least enable the identification of a cost ceiling? Unfortunately, this is also not the case: Such a cost ceiling would presuppose that you abstract completely from times and from the load in the business process model. In practice, this is completely unrealistic, since any consideration of business parameters is also coupled to a chronological consideration and the utilization of resources. Storage costs simply depend on the storage period, waiting times before processing steps result from the amount of pending work orders and the available resources, etc. In summary, therefore, it can be established that the simulation cannot be omitted if temporal aspects and process utilization are also to be considered.

Simulation requires mandatory support through a powerful modeling and simulation tool, of course, based on XML net simulation. To understand the methodological basis, it is necessary to realize how the defined business parameters are to be dealt with within the simulation. This is the only way to ensure that the parameters truly reflect the technical conditions accurately and calculate realistic simulation results based on this. Finally, it is indeed up to the user to interpret the results correctly and to draw the proper conclusions, for example, deriving optimization approaches.

For the following methodological discussion, we draw on an example from the leather goods production, which is shown in Fig. 4.29. The figure illustrates the activity of `Punching`, in which a `Work piece`—for simplicity reasons, the possibility of working with lots is abstracted from here—is processed into a `Punched part` with a `Punching machine`. The `Punching machine` itself is considered as a resource. For simplicity, the punching tool is missing here, the use of which in practice regularly has an especially large impact on cost and quality, often constituting the real capacity bottleneck. The tool could be either considered as a resource or as an object stored in an object store. The latter approach is preferred, although the tool creation takes place as part of the business process under examination. This small digression already shows that degrees of freedom in the context of the Horus method certainly exist that the modeler can use to simplify the models, but above all, to reflect the business requirements in a most precise and elegant manner.

The total cost of the `Punching` activity, with a one-time implementation, can then be calculated in simplified terms as follows:

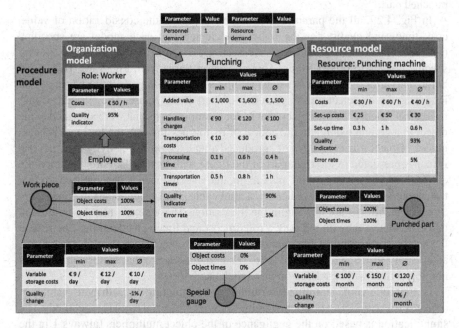

Fig. 4.29 Fragment of a business process model from the leather goods production

	Processing costs of activity (`Punching`)
+	Transport costs of activity (`Punching`)
+	Costs of used objects transferred (`Work piece`)
+	Usage fees transferred of objects read (`Special gauge`)
+	Personnel costs (`Worker`)
+	Resource costs (`Punching machine`) plus setup costs (`Punching machine`)
=	Total cost of the activity

Minimum, maximum, and average costs are then respectively determined during simulation. In calculating the personnel and resource costs, the requirements (in this case, both for the worker and the punching machine each equal to 1) must be respected. In connection with the cost transfer of object costs, object multipliers are to be taken into account (in the example, this is always 1) and the object cost parameters that determine the percentage of costs that are passed on to the consuming activity. In the example of the work piece, 100% of the costs are passed on, and for special gauges, 0%. The object cost parameters come into play even when it comes to the question of which part of the activity costs are to be passed on to the objects created. In the example, 100% of the costs will be passed on to the punched part.

In Fig. 4.29, all the parameters that are relevant to the consideration of value, cost, time, and quality for the individual elements of each model are specified (for an explanation of parameters, see Sect. 4.4.3). Not shown is the allocation of specific objects to object stores. This allocation arises from Fig. 4.30. The layout before and after the simulation steps is shown. The pending object to be processed is indicated with select attributes in the left part of the figure. The attribute values reflect the "history" of the object, that is, for example, costs that were allocated to the object to a certain extent "in the course of its journey through the business process model." Object `Punched part`, produced after execution of activity `Punching`, is then represented in the right part of the figure with its details. For simplicity, the distinction between minimum, maximum, and average values was omitted, so that the average value is always indicated, if applicable. The object details in object store `Special gauge` are missing in the illustration. These details may be omitted in this example, as they do not play a role in cost and time consideration. The reason lies in the parameters of the connection between object store `Special gauge` and activity `Punching` that are set to 0% and thus ensure that neither object costs nor object time will be passed on through the activity.

In the following, simplified formulas for calculating the attribute values of object `Punched part` after running activity `Punching` are specified. The simplification is based on the negligence of the object multipliers (always 1 in the example) as well as the number of employees and resources required (in the example also always 1) and the object costs or object time-parameter of `Punched part` (in

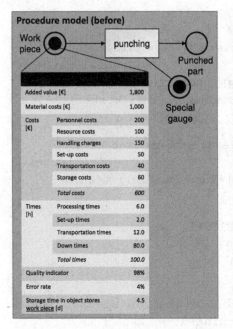
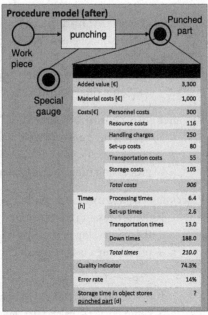

Fig. 4.30 Object allocation (marking) before and after a simulation

this case, always 100%). The corresponding parameters for objects `Work piece` (100%) and `Special gauge` (0%) are respectively specified. The calculation of the "punch part accumulated" value creation takes place according to the following formula:

Value creation (`Work piece`) =
100% value creation (`Work piece`) + 0% value creation
(`Special gauge`)
+ value creation (`Punching`)

The following calculation is based on the idea that the punched part is formed within activity `Punching` in input objects `Work piece` and `Special gauge`. The value creation of the activity is added to the existing accrued and pro rata (according to the object costs parameter of the connection) recharged value creation in the input objects. The material costs are as follows:

Material costs (`Punched part`) =
100% material costs (`Work piece`) + 0% material costs
(`Special gauge`)

This will be applied, considering assigned roles and resources, to the different types of costs:

Personnel costs (`Punched part`) =
   100% personnel costs (`Work piece`) + 0% personnel costs
                                             (`Special gauge`)
      + (processing time (`Punching`) + transport times (`Punching`)
         + Setup time (`Punching machine`)) ∗ costs (`Worker`)

Resource costs (`Punched Part`) =
   100% resource costs (`Work piece`) + 0% resource costs
                                             (`Special gauge`)
      + processing time (`Punching`) ∗ costs (`Punching machine`)

Processing costs (`Punched part`) =
   100% processing costs (`Work piece`)
      + 0% processing costs (`Special gauge`)
      + processing costs (`Punching`)

Setup costs (`Punched part`) =
   100% setup costs (`Work piece`) + 0% setup costs (`Special gauge`)
      + setup costs (`Punching machine`)

Transportation costs (`Punched part`) =
   100% transportation costs (`Work piece`) + 0% transportation costs
                                             (`Special gauge`)
      + Transportation costs (`Punching`)

Storage costs (`Punched part`) =
   100% (storage costs (`Work piece`) + storage period (`Work piece`)
      ∗ variable storage costs (`Work piece`)
      + 0% (storage costs (`Special gauge`) + storage period
                                             (`Special gauge`)
         ∗ variable storage costs (`Special gauge`))
      + Transportation costs (`Punching`)

An anomaly arises in the context of the storage period. This can always be determined only at the time of the removal of the object from the object store by forming the difference at the time of deposit.

One will proceed in a similar manner with the costs in calculating the various time components. The 100% or 0% does not arise from the object cost shares but from the object time shares:

Processing times (`Punching`) =
    100% processing times (`Work piece`)
    + 0% processing times (`Special gauge`)
    + processing time (`Punching`)

Setup times (`Punching`) =
    100% setup times (`Work piece`) + 0% setup times
                                            (`Special gauge`)
    + Setup time (`Punching machine`)

Transportation times (`Punching`) =
    100% transportation times (`Work piece`) + 0% transportation times
                                                    (`Special gauge`)
    + transportation times (`Punching`)

Down times (`Punching`) =
    100% (down times (`Work piece`) + storage period (`Work piece`))
    + 0% (down times (`Special gauge`) + storage period
                                            (`Special gauge`))

All influential factors flow together in calculating the quality indicators: the quality
of the objects used, the quality of the activity, and the quality provided by the
personnel and the resources used. Concerning the object quality, it is important to
note that the actual quality cannot be calculated until the date of use, because only
then do storage time and the overall quality change stand certain.

Quality indicator (`Punching`) =
    (Quality indicator (`Work piece`)
      + Storage period (`Work piece`) * quality change (`Work piece`))
    * (Quality indicator (`Special gauge`)
      + Storage period (`Special gauge`) * quality change
                                            (`Special gauge`))
    * quality indicator (`Punching`)
    * quality indicator (`Worker`) * quality indicator
                                            (`Punching machine`)

The error rate arises from summation of the error rates of the objects with the error
rates of the activity and the resources. The object costs and object-time parameters
do not play a role when considering the quality and error rates.

4.4.5 Analysis of Simulation Runs

The previous explanations for simulation underline the significance of simulation
for effective business process engineering. They also make it clear that the amount
of resulting runtime data in the context of the simulation requires a powerful

repository. The reporting and analysis of the runtime data also calls for flexible business intelligence technologies, which also quickly and easily satisfy individual information needs.

This being said, the Horus method demands an integrated repository where all runtime data of the simulation are stored with the model data. This repository will form the basis for simple reports and analyses as needed to visualize the procedures involved in the animation. For an analysis that is more complex or for individual user requests, the object-relational structured repository is only of limited suitability and quickly reaches its limits particularly in terms of flexibility, ease of use, and efficiency. For this reason, the model and runtime data deposited in the repository are provided in addition to optimized data storage for analytical processing called a data mart. A data mart is based on a multidimensional data model, in which the facts (in this case the transition operations) are separated from the dimensions and stored (in this example, activities, roles, resources). This allows a fast and flexible analysis of large data bases. The visualization of data and analysis results takes place in structured reports, online spreadsheets, and business graphics as well as in interactive dashboards. Of particular interest are a comparative analysis of different simulation types and the subsequent comparison with benchmarks that are predefined for certain types of processes and industries.

A more detailed description of the technical implementation possibilities will not be covered in this book. The following statements therefore concentrate primarily on the evaluation possibilities required as a part of the Horus method. These are classified and the classes will be explained based on important and typical expressions.

4.4.5.1   Analysis of Activations and Transition Firings

Activities

The usage profile of an activity can be determined from the transition occurrences in a simple manner: How often and when was it activated and how often and when was it actually executed? The *work in process* immediately follows from the number of activations, which is available for a particular activity. Anomalies often arise from a high share of cases in which an activity was activated but has not been executed. Such cases require a more detailed examination, supported by drill-down capabilities. Of particular interest are reports where the transition operations are associated with time attributes: The distribution of handling, transportation, setup (derived from the use of resources), and waiting times can be determined for each activity over the entire simulation period. Corresponding aggregate statements for individually prepared sets of activities can also be won for the whole network or the entire process, of course. This applies to all targeted evaluations. Just by considering the transition procedures, existing activity-based statements concerning the value as well as a cost analysis with distribution to processing and transportation, human resources (derived from role use), and setup costs (derived from the use of resources) are possible.

Object Stores

A usage profile can be created for object stores analogously to the activities. However, this usually has a lower significance for the practitioner; also, the links to simulation time, which would be indirectly possible through the time attributes of the related activities, are generally omitted. Particularly interesting, however, is the study of conflict situations that have arisen in that several activities are competing for the objects of an input object store or for the free capacity of a shared output object store. The analysis results provide important information on consequences of capacity expansions.

Roles and Employees

Usage profiles can be created at both role and employee level, which in this context are appropriately described as *activity profiles*. Furthermore, it can be evaluated how the working hours are allocated to processing, transportation and setup tasks, and the waiting times incurred as a result thereof. This easily allows statements concerning the utilization of existing personnel resources to be made as well as the derivation of work in process over time. Moreover, evaluations of personnel expenditures "passed on" to the activities are possible.

Resources

Regarding resources, the same evaluations are relevant as in the case of the roles. Detailed statements about setup times and costs are also possible.

4.4.5.2   Analysis of States

States, that is, the markings of nets over time, are already subject to an analytical consideration in connection with the transition procedures. Moreover, they are in the center of the interest in the known Petri net analysis. At this point, another state-related analysis will be addressed, relating to object store allocation.

Object Store Allocation

The allocation of object stores over time—with particular reference to peak capacities—provides interesting insights into the workload and thus the required capacities; whether warehouse or memory capacities, or even necessary resources, if these have been modeled in the net in terms of objects. In most cases, the overview of the allocation of object stores as a starting point is used for detailed examinations (drill down) of the specifically stored objects.

4.4.5.3   Analysis of Objects

Value and Cost Analysis

In many practical applications, value and cost analysis up to complete activity-based costing stands at the center of attention. The corresponding numerical data can be recovered over time by examining the contents of the object stores. The stored items carry detailed cost information to enable a breakdown of costs-by-cost element and the comparison with the achieved added value. Maximum and minimum values as well as expected value distributions and variance statements can be obtained from the considered objects. Feasible cost aggregations and selections round off the spectrum of analysis.

Time-Based Analysis

An analysis of time-related attributes which the objects carry is also intended analogously to cost considerations. How are processing, setup, transportation, and downtimes distributed and what are the minimum and maximum values?

Quality Analysis

The quality indicators and error rates which the objects carry are considered in the context of the object analysis. Here again, proven statistical methods are applied to come to such valuable statements about the quality of the objects generated.

4.5   Business Process Management and Process Implementation

Business process engineering provides solutions primarily to the difficult problem of converting business requirements accurately and completely into a world of models, in order to make them accessible to formal analysis. Moreover, without abstract models, it is rarely possible to maintain discussions on business requirements at a business level without digressing into issues of actual implementation. Undoubtedly, such a digression can also be used specifically as a tool for a case-oriented communication of business requirements; however, this requires moderation which leads the discussion back to the abstract model level at an appropriate point.

The benefits of modeling, however, can only develop fully when the models meet certain key criteria:

- They must be designed in such a way that they are easy to understand for the particular business department, yet at the same time, they must be accessible for automated quality assurance tools.
- They must offer structuring possibilities that will still keep the models clear, even if the facts are complex and extensive.
- As if this was not yet enough, the concept of a holistic business process management (BPM) moves into the foreground—driven by the ongoing paradigm shift in IT to service-oriented architecture (SOA). At the same time, this involves concepts and methodical specifications for an implementation of the modeled business processes.

The Horus method meets this last claim with a consistent approach that flows into service-oriented business process management architecture.

4.5.1 Business Process Management Within the Horus Method

Figure 4.31 illustrates the Horus Business Process Management (BPM) architecture, which spans the range from a strategic consideration of the enterprise down to

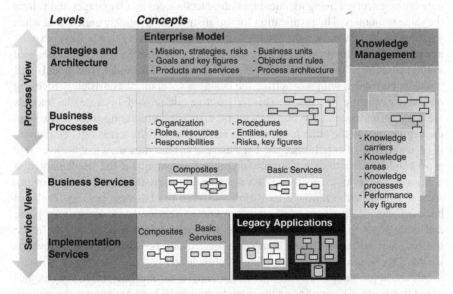

Fig. 4.31 Business process management within the Horus method

practical implementation. To this end, the architecture has four description levels. It would be ideal if this complex structure level could be dispensed with and a concrete implementation in the form of information systems and organizational arrangements could directly be derived from the enterprise model at a strategy and architectural level. Unfortunately, the complexity of such a mapping process is way too high: Too many and too unsafe design decisions must be made, for which the most part absolutely no basis for a decision even exists. So what remains is to reduce the complexity by introducing additional description levels. In addition, methods and software tools—Horus is a typical representative in this case—see to it that the effort required can be kept low and quality problems can be avoided wherever possible.

In the preceding sections of this chapter, it has been shown which possibilities the Horus method offers to build business models at a *strategy and architecture level*. It also describes a path from this enterprise model to a comprehensive *business process model*. Consistently applied, it will provide a full process view of the business requirements to be considered. In terms of holistic business process management, only a part of the path has been traveled at this point, however, since the goal is to transform the business processes and enterprise model requirements into an implementation with maximum coverage. For that purpose, the Horus BPM architecture provides two additional layers that first allow a transition to a service view via the business service level and hereafter to the IT—as well as organizational implementation.

While the need for an *implementation services layer* is obvious, the question arises as to the importance of an explicit *business services layer*. So far, business process models were always addressed in connection with business models. In fact, business service models are only a specific type of business process models, that is, they are constructed using identical modeling techniques and languages and follow the same semantics. The justification for this distinction is quickly understood when you look at the (often-encountered) practical case, considering that business experts and process consultants, who more or less consciously abstract from the subsequent implementation of the processes, create a business process model. The models will typically be riddled with words from the business vocabulary, consistently focusing on subject-specific processes. This is positive all around because the models are easy to understand for business users, primarily addressing these right from the beginning. On the other hand, models are needed which increasingly emphasize implementation-oriented concepts: The business terminology used and the available processes and structures are more generalized, especially if the implementation is done via a packaged software that is offered in various sectors. The following section will describe how the transitions between the business process level and business service level, up to the implementation service level, are to take place and what motivation the two-step implementation approach is based on. In the illustration, basic services and composite services are possible at both the level of business services as well as the implementation level.

A central problem of business process management must be pointed out explicitly at this point. As tempting as the thought may be to have an integrated approach of strategic considerations up to executable information systems, be warned against overestimating the performance of the instruments used in BPM. Still, the mapping of business requirements in the BPM world is by far the most difficult problem. Methods and tools such as Horus can provide a valuable service, but should not be seen as a comprehensive cure, as it is still the individual person that stands at the heart of this imaging process with his communication, abstraction and structuring skills, and—not to be underestimated—his or her creativity. Furthermore, the transition from a process view to a service view should not be denoted as trivial (more on that later). The BPM architecture must also deal with ongoing changes, both in business and its environment as well as in the implementation itself. It is also a challenge to keep all descriptions across all levels consistent and complete—the only way BPM can really be of use. This issue has to be addressed by technical means and will also have to meet with organizational regulations.

One key to the efficient use of BPM is offered by *knowledge management*—an indispensable component of any BPM architecture in the Horus method. It is obvious why this is the case: Knowledge management enables the people involved in BPM to work effectively and to fulfill their tasks in high quality. It describes fields of knowledge and helps to structure and administer this knowledge in an appropriate manner and to pinpoint sources of knowledge. Automated knowledge processes and key performance indicators bring efficiency into knowledge management and offer assistance in the acquisition of additional knowledge inside and outside of the organization.

4.5.2 Abstract Implementation of Business Processes

The majority of BPM solutions that can be found in the market today place the execution of business processes at the center of their consideration. This is obvious at first glance, as the greatest optimization potential will be expected here. This is especially true if the execution environment is a service-oriented architecture. The objective of such an architecture is to lower implementation costs by providing reusable services and their orchestration to comprehensive processes while achieving high-quality results. With this optimization potential in mind, modeling languages are propagated at the business process level, allowing a simple and ideally bidirectional mapping of business processes in an executable form. A typical example is BPMN, the *Business Process Modeling Notation* of the Object Management Group (OMG), which is capable of providing a simple and efficiently automatable implementation in BPEL processes (BPEL is an acronym for *Business Process Execution Language*). An implementation of BPEL structures back to BPMN can be easily accomplished, so that changes to implemented BPEL processes in the BPMN models can follow. In this context, one speaks of a *round trip* that makes the consistency preservation between different levels of BPM architecture much easier.

As convincing as this approach may sound, it nonetheless holds serious draw-backs, as the possibility of a bidirectional mapping of the respective models comes at the expense that the professional business modeling language is oriented toward the requirements of a future implementation. The business community must therefore become familiar with aspects of a subsequent implementation. More concretely, the discussion suddenly turns toward control structures and loop termination criteria and the like; the focus on business often goes offtrack in this case. Moreover, it is clear that the decision concerning the nature of the subsequent implementation of the business process always has a significant impact on the content of the business process model. It becomes very dangerous when these aspects that cannot be "programmed" into the target system also do not find themselves within the business process model—organizational rules and responsibilities, constraints, and economic goals, just to name a few.

The Horus method follows a completely different path here, because the abstraction of implementation issues represents a very important requirement for a modeling procedure that should be applicable for all members of the business community. However, the opportunities for an automation of business process implementation and for round trips are constrained by this, and they are replaced by interactive, wizard-based transformation steps. The transition from the business process level of the Horus BPM architecture to the business service level, which also means a change from the process view to a service point of view, is referred to as *abstract implementation* in the Horus method; abstract because an abstraction from the technical implementation consciously takes place. Notably, the transition to the business service level ensues even if the implementation to a legacy environment takes place. A virtualization obviously takes place here, where a virtual execution level in the form of business services is placed through the specific execution level. The advantages are obvious: Changes in the system environment—such as the change from one business software to another or switching from a client/server to a service-oriented architecture—can be easily comprehended, often with no change in the business service layer.

Figure 4.32 shows the concepts of the abstract implementation in the Horus method. The key is the *business process implementation model*. Formally, it represents a set of XML nets that refine the activities of the business process model. The initially obvious top-down refinement generally does not lead to the desired objective, as it would prevent the change of perspective of the business processes to the business services. A structuring of the abstract business service layer must therefore first be carried out in the context of the framework of requirements targeted by the business process models. Structuring elements are costs, periods of time, standards to be complied with (compliance), controllability (governance), technical feasibility, and the objective of the highest possible degree of reutilization. The resulting structure forms the framework for the orchestration of business services in the business process implementation model. The next section will describe how this orchestration is to be carried out.

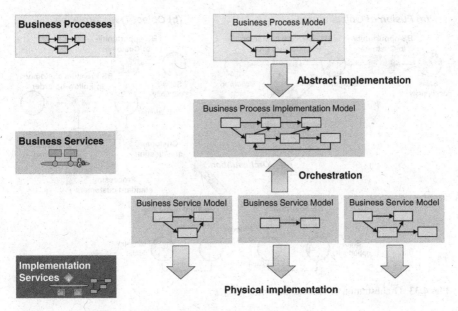

Fig. 4.32   Abstract implementation and business service orchestration

4.5.3   Orchestration of Business Services

The orchestration of business services can easily be thought of as an "assembly" of multiple business service models. Models can be connected directly to each other, just as with assembly in the usual manner, if they exhibit the appropriate object stores or activities. "Compatibility" does not necessarily mean that the model elements are also identically designated—much more important is that they are of the same type and exhibit identical semantics. Clear descriptions within the business service models are required to recognize this, particularly with respect to the input and output object stores.

The two business services Premium customer-to-Follow-up order and Opportunity-to-Customer are depicted in the lower area of Fig. 4.33. For simplicity, they are graphically illustrated as dashed boxes, indicating the interface object store. A direct connection is shown with respect to object store Customer in Fig. 4.33a: Input object store Premium customer of business service Premium customer-to-Follow-up order and Opportunity-to-Customer matches the output object store Customer of business service Opportunity-to-Customer and can therefore be fused together during orchestration. To "match," however, does not necessarily mean that the elements have the same name—as in this example. In the example, therefore, object store Premium customer was renamed to Customer for the fusion. It is also necessary to provide the activity BS Premium customer-to-Follow-up order with a constraint in the orchestrated

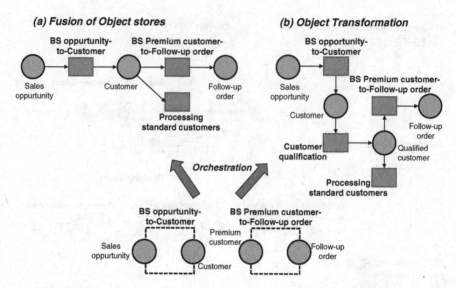

Fig. 4.33 Orchestration of business services

model (such as annual revenues > EUR 1 million), which ensures that only premium customers are actually processed.

To complete this, an activity is then added which processes nonpremium customers. Even this small example shows that orchestration can very well be a creative process.

The orchestration takes place by inserting an intermediate structure, as shown in Fig. 4.33b. This ensures the transformation of object store `Customer` to `Qualified customer`. This qualification activity expands the customer object with attributes, qualifying it as a premium or regular customer. With orchestration it often occurs, of course, that entire process chains must be newly inserted. Furthermore, the need for new or amended business services arises.

4.5.4   Physical Implementation of Business Services

Virtualization, which is implemented during abstract business process implementation, undoubtedly offers great advantages when abstracting from aspects of a specific physical implementation of services. In terms of a holistic BPM approach, it merely defers the problem to a deeper level. It must be correctly noted, however, that the deferral is accompanied by a drastic reduction in the complexity of the implementation. In addition, with the consistent use of the Horus method in connection with Horus Best Practice Models (see Sect. 4.6), it will often be the case that business service models used in the virtualization layer will also include complete physical implementations. This type of reutilization provides high efficiency, of course.

The most significant forms of physical implementation of business services will be briefly described in the following. What all methods have in common is that they should be combined with measures for the ongoing review of business performance, building upon this with key figure-based business process management. Topic discussions can be found in Sect. 4.5.5.

4.5.4.1 Organizational Directives

Perhaps the most important type of business service implementation remains in the form of *organizational directives*. The ideal case is that the enterprise can agree on the models created with Horus as a binding organizational directive. The models are then made available to the employees in personalized form on a Web process portal (see Sect. 4.5.5). The integration of external process partners (customers, business partners, suppliers, etc.) can also be carried out via Web portals. It is particularly effective when the models are provided in context-sensitive form: When completing a particular task, the exact information is then made available relevant to the context of that task.

The fact that efficient business processes cannot be realized by exclusively utilizing a "conservative" implementation of business processes across organizational instructions is obvious. Nevertheless, there are valid reasons to include such a conservative procedure during implementation. These range from budget considerations up to and including the preclusion of labor disputes. Often an evolutionary change management process also includes a gradual arming of business process automation, complemented by organizational directives.

4.5.4.2 Conventional Implementation in a Legacy Environment

What may seem strange at first glance makes a great deal of sense in the context of a future-oriented IT strategy: Although strongly function-oriented monolithic IT applications are still being used within the enterprise, the application landscape is already being structured in the form of business services. The path to a service-oriented future is opened early on, making a gradual transition toward the new paradigm of service orientation possible. Besides, this is the path most often encountered in practice. During the implementation of business services in a legacy environment, one must understand that important aspects that are explicitly deposited within the business service model—consider, for example, procedure control, responsibilities, or business rules—are "hardwired" within legacy environments. Thus, the transparency and easy modification that is typical for services, or the reutilization during implementation, are lost. It can, however, be reproduced at any time during the possible subsequent transition toward service orientation from the business service model.

Table 4.1 Allocation of SOA components to Horus models

Horus model		SOA component
Process model	→	Service bus and BPEL process management
Business units and organization model	→	Identity management
Resource model, competencies, and areas of responsibility	→	Identity and BPEL process management
Object and entity model	→	Master data management, operational and analytical databases
Rule model	→	Business rule management
Objective, strategy, and key figures model	→	Business activity and performance management

4.5.4.3 Implementation in a Service-Oriented Architecture

Service-oriented architecture (SOA) allows a natural form of business service implementation (see Sect. 5.2). This means that the majority of professional business modeling constructs also find a correlation in SOA methodologies and tools. This does not apply to all modeling attributes, so that a certain amount of organizational instructions cannot be dispensed with even in a SOA. Note also that there is no 1 : 1 correlation between the business service established at a more business level and the service implementation: A basic service in the business service model, for example, may require many implementation service composites for its implementation.

Table 4.1 lists where Horus models can be found in an SOA implementation.

4.5.4.4 Introduction of Packaged Application Software

New technologies and paradigms in IT regularly demand new models and approaches, including the implementation of packaged application software,[2] such as SAP, Oracle Applications, or Microsoft Dynamics. Model-driven approaches to defining and implementing such software systems are required. Furthermore, it has become apparent that the rising market demand for service-oriented solutions is pushing even large producers in this direction. Up to now, the introduction of

---

[2]Here, we use the term "packaged application software" commonly used in practice. This term is actually wrong because in the area of business application software (business software), there can really be no standard application software—the professional requirements of corporate users vary too much in this respect. The term "configurable software" would be more accurate, because it can be adapted to specific user needs, such as personalization, parameters, workflows, rules, or other techniques.

standard software has taken place in the context of traditional software engineering, starting from a requirements analysis up to the go live of the system. The modeling of business processes to be implemented as part of the requirements analysis provides the basis for the design and architecture of the system. A problem with this approach to the introduction of standard software is the deviation of the company-specific business processes from the prescribed processes of standard application software. The approach of a multilayer model, such as that used in the Horus method, allows a degree of abstraction-based representation of business services, that is, the functionality of standard software at different levels. Business process models in conjunction with business service models, as provided for by the Horus method, reduce complexity and enable flexible business process management through the orchestration of business services. These can be combined horizontally with comprehensive business processes, linking them to one another vertically through refinements. An implementation of these processes is possible based on the industry-standard BPEL, which is already being used in many standard software products for system integration.

4.5.5 Business Process Portals and Business Performance Management

Horus Business Process Management is based on three principles, which are reflected not only in the BPM architecture but also in the methods and the software tools provided:

- *Participation*: Integration of the entire business community into the design and use of business process models as well as exchange across community boundaries.
- *Transparency*: Substantial disclosure of business process models and business process knowledge as well as identification of knowledge carriers. Monitoring of business performance and key-figure-based process control.
- *Ongoing improvement*: Participation and transparency set the stage for the ongoing improvement of business processes. Simulation studies provide a strong basis for what-if analysis and the comparison of process variations.

As plausible as these principles may appear, they are very difficult to achieve in practice and quite often against considerable resistance by the affected organization. A strong participation of the business community simply leads to the emancipation of the business department and, subsequently, often to considerable demands on quality and volume of requested IT services. Not every user and business department is actually interested in full transparency with respect to efficiency and performance. In addition, labor law conditions must not be overlooked here. Finally, budget limits often stand against the demand for an ongoing improvement of business processes as well as user rejection by "those who have always done it this way."

These remarks make it clear that business process management not only requires methods and tools but exceedingly an effective preparation and implementation of organizational change: Change management is success factor no. 1 in business process management!

A very important change management tool are *business process portals* which enable an efficient and cost-effective business community integration. Figure 4.34 shows the typical structure of such a business process portal. It is based on a repository in which the model data and connections to the runtime environment are defined. Automated processes ensure ongoing monitoring of business performance and effective management of escalations based on key figures within the business process management. Different user groups will be integrated through personalization with the goal of optimal usability: management and employees (B2E—business-to-employee), different business partners (B2B—business-to-business), business and private customers (B2C—business-to-consumer), and, increasingly, public authorities (B2G—business-to-government). It should be noted that in B2B and B2G, concepts must frequently be implemented in which the contents of the business process and business process management portal must be made available on external partner portals. Similarly, mobile portals found especially on PDAs, handheld computers, and "smart mobile" phones are common practice these days.

A fundamental part of process portals are *portlets* for business performance management: Key figure values are visualized, compared with comparative data and analyzed over time in the form of *dashboards* and *scorecards*. A performance-based business process management is realized in conjunction with automated escalation mechanisms and on-line analysis. *Collaboration functionalities* are indispensable

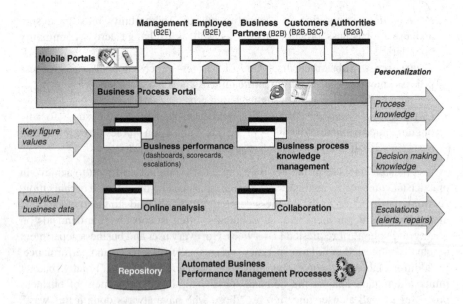

Fig. 4.34 Typical structure of a business process portal

as well, which make a Web-based collaboration within the business community possible in the first place. Today's demands go far beyond e-mail and instant messaging and include all common social networking features. Business process knowledge management completes the spectrum of the process portal by providing opportunities to flexibly retrieve, connect, and evaluate the model information stored in the repository to create a knowledge basis, forging the prerequisites for effective participation of all members of the business community.

When is the best time to set up a business process portal? The most obvious and easiest way would be to implement the portal on the final BPM solution. This approach would also be advocated from a cost perspective. Interesting utilization effects would then be given away, however, as has been proven in practice. It is preferable to set up an initial version of the portal at the beginning of a BPM project. Thus, the "habituation effect" relative to BPM thinking sets in at an early stage, especially if little potential for conflict has arisen. This portal will be updated—using an appropriate approval process, of course—with current business process models, which are then made available to the business community. Participation will be applied using collaboration features to further develop the models, stimulating true innovative processes wherever possible. This openness may be surprising, and enterprises must usually be introduced to it gradually, but it often sets untapped knowledge potential free within the organization. It is also interesting to first measure in the portal actual key figures in order to obtain comparative values with extensive explanatory power in the final measurement of success for the BPM project.

4.6   Best Practice and Reference Models

This book repeatedly points out the benefits that come along with working with business process models. As obvious as these benefits may be, the effort connected with model building should not be underestimated. As with learning a foreign language, the efforts connected with the use of a modeling language subsides with increasing modeler experience. Modeling becomes particularly efficient when the modeler begins to think in terms of the modeling language. He or she then has the experience to question business matters at detail level and from different angles in interviews, workshops, and document analyses so that he or she can represent them within the model thoroughly in a "natural" manner.

Nevertheless, other techniques become necessary that make effective model usage possible, especially within enterprise-wide projects. The Horus method provides for the design of a model library, making proven and trusted models available for reuse. This involves models that have been proven in practice or even define an industry standard (see Sect. 5.1.4). In practice, terms such as *best practice models* or *reference models* are used, although the terms are not clearly separated from one another.

In this book, we consider reference models as a subset of best practice models. This is done in light of the principle of reuse, yielding the desired productivity gains within the modeling work with high model quality as a desired side effect. A distinction is made between planned and unplanned reuse in this regard. During the intended reuse, the models are conceptualized for future use—such as by structure or configuration and exceptional quality; unplanned reuse obeys the principle of contingency. It therefore carries the risk that not only the desired model fragments but also mistakes and shortcomings can be reused. Moreover, not all specifically designed models are suitable for reuse and may show incorrect facts in a foreign context.

In the following, we speak of best practice models whenever we assume reuse in general terms. On the other hand, we presuppose a planned reuse for reference models. Special requirements are applied against its contents, it must be clear in what context, and under what conditions they may be used. Moreover, it must be indicated in what manner they are configured. A term that finds use in this context is the *knowledge base*. In the context of the Horus method, one speaks in general of a knowledge base when artifacts of all kinds—not just models or model fragments but also program modules, etc.—are made available for reuse.

The reutilization techniques included in the Horus method will be shown below. These techniques can always be used to develop best practice model libraries. And they also form the basis for the Horus Knowledge Bases™.

The Horus method knows two types of best practice models: *business process models* and *business service models*. It falls back to the concept presented in Sect. 4.5.1 of business process management (BPM) in the Horus method: Business process models are used at the level of business objectives and strategies as well as on the actual business process level. Business service models create the transition to the level of business services, that is, ultimately to process implementation.

The examples of best practice models given below could lead to the conclusion that such models are always procedure models. This conclusion is incorrect and stems from a simplified subject matter presentation, as best practice models can include all model aspects that the Horus method has to offer. This is used extensively in practice. Apart from that, there are best practice models that contain absolutely no procedures, but only business objects or organization structures.

4.6.1 Industry Business Process Models

In the Horus method, business process models always pursue the goal of a common understanding at a business level. As a result, they use a current vocabulary and are oriented toward business conditions in their processes and structures. Specific terms are often given preference over more general, generic names and descriptions. In this respect, it is not possible to offer best practice business models that would possess validity for each application area and possibly an entire economic sector—they would be far too generic and would have to be elaborately adapted and customized in the case of actual use. On the other hand, best practice business process models should not just cover one specific application but an entire class of such cases. For these reasons, the Horus method provides industry business process models, that is, models based on the needs of a clearly defined target group—of the respective industry sector.

With this, the Horus method follows considerations that various industry or business associations have already implemented into appropriate reference models. Examples include the *enhanced Telecom Operations Map®* (eTOM® for short) of the TeleManagement Forum and the SCOR® *Supply Chain Operations Reference Model* by the Supply Chain Council. Both reference models are presented in Sect. 5.1.4.

The Horus method proposes the structure shown in Fig. 4.35 for the creation of a best practice business process model. The left side of the illustration shows the relevant levels of the Horus Business Process Management concept. They allow an assignment of various model levels in the BPM concept.

Following Horus method fundamentals, the best practice model first offers a *context model* in order to make a placement into the intended target application field possible. Next, the *business process architecture model* provides an overview of the business processes contained in the best practice model. These are then refined respectively in a multilevel hierarchy of *business process models*. Level 1 models each describe a core process. This can be an entire division (e.g., green biotechnology in a life science company) or only a main task, for example, customer service. Level 2 refines the core process activities, such as field service in this example. The refinement then closes frequently with Level 3, in which the activities are mostly refined to the level of *business transactions*, for example, Order spare part. This level of refinement is often quite sufficient if one once again understands that the implementation is then provided in the form of abstract business

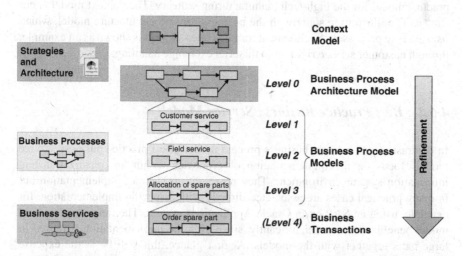

Fig. 4.35 Structure of best practice business process models according to the Horus method

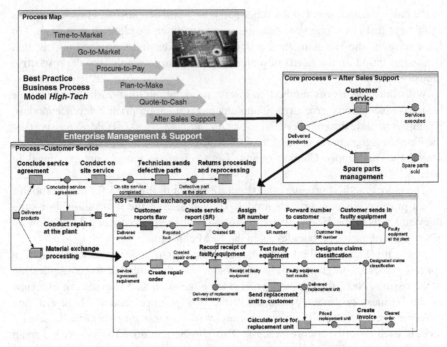

Fig. 4.36 Extract of a best practice business process model

services. In the illustration, an example of a business service `Order spare part` is given to illustrate the transition to business service level.

The application of the described concept is shown in Fig. 4.36 based on an extract from a professionally applied industry business process model. This is a best practice model for the high-tech manufacturing industry. The context model is not shown. The illustration starts with the business process architecture model, which lists the core processes. A refinement for after sales support is shown as an example, through customer service right up to material exchange handling.

4.6.2 Best Practice Business Service Models

In contrast to the industry business process models, best practice business service models focus on the implementation of processes within an organization and information system environment. They represent an abstract implementation but in many practical cases are associated directly with a specific implementation, for example, using an SAP or an Oracle Applications system. The range of reuse and model benefits then rises significantly, since even the implementation is reused in large parts together with the models. At first glance, this will be at the expense of application breadth, which, however, is contradicted by many successful case studies: Due to the similarities between application software products, resulting from many years of competition, the reuse of a business service model with an underlying Oracle Applications implementation provides for beneficial effects even when an SAP or Microsoft Dynamics solution is introduced.

Although a late implementation plays an important role in business service models, mediation of a common understanding of the respective processes and associated functionalities of the business service stands in the foreground. The models also serve as a central communications instrument between all parties involved in the project, in particular between the user and the application solution implementer. Considerable requirements on model clarity and precision arise from this. Ready-made best practice models can score with excellent quality here, thus becoming a project accelerator.

Figure 4.37 shows the structure of a best practice business service model as provided for in the Horus method. The left side of the illustration depicts the relevant levels of the Horus method BPM concept for the classification of model levels. The model tree root usually—but not necessarily, because the Horus method also provides atomic best practice business services—forms a model of a *composite business service*, that is, a business service that is created by orchestrating various basic business services. The composite business service can also be perceived as a *business flow* to establish the relationship with other modeling techniques. The basic business services are completely modeled at Level 1. These can also be used independently of the composite service as an abstract implementation of a business process. Level 2 provides an overview of the process which forms the core of the basic business service. Level 3 shows how this is created by an orchestration of subprocesses. It should be noted at this point that the specification depth of a best

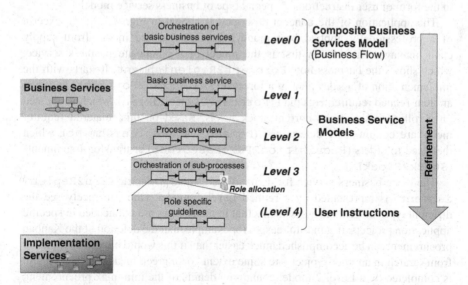

Fig. 4.37 Structure of best practice business service models in the Horus method

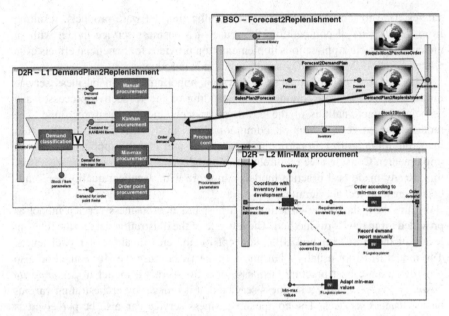

Fig. 4.38 Extract from a best practice business service model

practice model is an empirical value which can vary in practice entirely, especially if very simple or very complex and comprehensive services to be processed.

As a rule, role assignments are made in Level 3 to define responsibilities. It also makes sense to model detailed specifications for role tasks. This occurs at Level 4 in the form of user instructions, a special type of business service model.

The application of the concept described is shown in Fig. 4.38 in an excerpt of a professionally applied best practice business service model from supply chain management. Shown first is the model of a composite business service, which shows the business flow Forecast2Replenishment. It starts with the implementation of a sales plan in a forecast (SalesPlan2Forecast) and then an item-related requirements plan (Forecast2DemandPlan), which is updated on a rolling basis of the current stock levels. Based on this, material requirements are continuously determined (DemandPlan2Replenishment), which then lead to orders (Requisition2PurchaseOrder) or transfer assignments (Stock2Stock).

The basic business service for demand assessment (DemandPlan2Replenishment) is represented by a refined Level 1 model. One can nicely see the different types of demand assessments that in many cases are not needed in specific application projects. It stands to reason, for example, that the deletion of the Kanban procurement can be accomplished much easier than if this would have to be modeled from scratch in another project—to some extent "on a green meadow." The picture is completed by a Level 2 model containing details of the min–max procurement. There are activities in this model that are labeled with IN! This means that role-specific guidelines in the form of a *user instruction* lie behind this activity. In this simple example, the transition to the user instructions already takes place in Level 3 and not Level 4.

4.7   Self-Control

Exercise 4.1. Once again, understand the procedure of the Horus Business Process Engineering Method:

- Of what phases does the method consist of?
- What needs to be done in the course of a context analysis? Why does the Horus method start with this?
- What do Phases 1 and 2 of the Horus method have to provide?
- What are the drivers to perform a simulation?
- How do you go from completed business process models to implementation?
- What is the role of reference models?

Refer to Fig. 4.1 if necessary. In this context, recall the Horus method in your own words.

Exercise 4.2. Explain the four aspects of a SWOT analysis. Compare SWOT analysis and Balanced Scorecard. Which valuation method is preferable under what conditions? Perform a context and then a SWOT analysis for the case study `Power supplier` (see Exercise 3.1).

Exercise 4.3. Look again at Exercise 3.1, the preparation and examination of an application for credit with a bank. Apply the Horus method to this simple example. Go through all stages of the method, indicating each phase result. In Phase 2, place particular emphasis on the procedure and risk analysis.

Exercise 4.4. Create an industry business process model for a stationary trade business. How must this model change if you want to transfer it to electronic commerce?

4.8   Bibliographic References and Web Links

A great deal of literature exists concerning the topics of business process modeling and business process management, both in book form and in the form of numerous original papers. BPM methods and methodologies with a similar objective comparable to the Horus method are described, for example, by Weske (2007) or Scheer et al. (2002), where the former is based on BPMN (with the consequences and limitations discussed above) and the latter on ARIS, the *ARchitecture of integrated Information Systems*; for ARIS, see also Davis (2001, 2008) or Davis and Brabander (2007).

As mentioned in Sect. 4.5, the majority of BPM solutions encountered in the market today, however, place the execution of business processes in the center of their focus; as should be clear in this chapter, the Horus method goes far beyond that.

The concept of the Balanced Scorecard falls back on the work of Kaplan and Norton (1992, 1993). There are numerous citations on this subject, including Kaplan and Norton (1996, 2000, 2008).

An introduction to SWOT analysis is given by Fine (2009). Vose (2008) deals with the topic of risk analysis more precisely. An introduction to the field of simulation can be found in Ross (2006) or in Sokolowski and Banks (2009).

Business rules, consisting of events, conditions, and actions are closely related to event-condition-action (ECA) rules used in active databases; to this end, the reader is referred to Garcia-Molina et al. (2008) or to Silberschatz et al. (2010).

There are many other modeling methods and tools to be found on the web, including the following:

- For BPMN: www.visual-paradigm.com/solution/bpmodeling
- Signavio Process Editor:
  signavio.com/de/produkte/process-editor-as-a-service.html
- ARIS Express: www.ariscommunity.com/aris-express

Chapter 5
Areas of Application

Business processes are the focal point when it comes to changes in an enterprise. Be it the implementation of new business models and strategies, be it in the realization of information systems, or be it related to quality improvements—the discussion always involves business processes. As a logical consequence follows the necessity for a realistic and easy to understand portrayal of the business processes that qualify as a basis not only for effective communication but also for analysis and simulation. The models and methods covered in this book fully satisfy these requirements. Based on current practical projects, this chapter will show how the models can be used in important applications as well as the resulting benefits derived there from.

As varied as the applications are, one can always identify a model-centric project cycle as shown in Fig. 5.1. A structured, process-oriented target environment—already known from Sect. 4.6—can be found in the center of the illustration, around which the project cycle revolves. The structure and development of this environment is carried out with the help of suitable models, whereby the business process models form the central reference point.

The project cycle starts with an analysis of business requirements, culminating in a business as well as a technical concept. This will then form the starting point for an implementation in the form of organizational measures, in connection with the allocation of information technology systems. The efficiency of the implemented concept can be reviewed in the context of key process indicator monitoring. Based on ongoing changes, not only external factors or occurring risks but also opportunities can be quickly recognized with appropriate action then being taken. Sustainable changes require a specific analysis, in many cases involving an evolution of business processes, thus resulting in the cyclical project structure.

The application fields discussed in the following are characterized by a special relevance to the consideration of business processes. It will become clear that the above-mentioned model-centric project cycle can be found in all cases. Some of the applications have industry-specific features, which may limit the general applicability or may require an adaptation to industry specifications. These cases will be explicitly mentioned.

F. Schönthaler et al., *Business Processes for Business Communities*,
DOI 10.1007/978-3-642-24791-0_5, © Springer-Verlag Berlin Heidelberg 2012

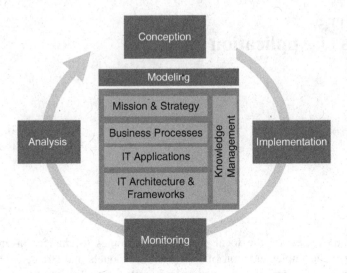

Fig. 5.1 Model-centered project cycle

5.1   Business Process Reengineering

Many books have been written on business process reengineering, some of which are listed in the Bibliographic Notes at the end of this chapter (or previous chapters). Genuine progress reports are rare, however. Why is this the case? Because the nature of business process reengineering is a "fundamental rethinking and redesigning of all business processes of an enterprise or corporate division." And as an objective, "dramatic and sustained improvements in process performance in terms of quality, cost, and time" come into question. The enterprises quickly find enthusiasm for this goal; however, they have trouble with fundamental rethinking and, above all, with an implementation of completely redesigned processes. This is particularly true when—and this is typical for business process reengineering—a new organization structure is derived from the new process. In practice, business process reengineering can only be successful in connection with an effective organizational change management. This shows that business process reengineering not only requires organizational strength in implementation but an "adequately dimensioned" project budget as well. In this respect, business process reengineering often comes too late for enterprises that already find themselves in an economic crisis. On the other hand, the approach is seen with special interest in emerging economies, such as the Middle and Far East and some Eastern European countries.

5.1.1   Drivers and External Factors

Cost savings are a desired side effect in business process reengineering (BPR); they are, however, unsuitable as a sole driver. Successful BPR projects are characterized by the fact that they are driven by the desire for optimal performance of the entrepreneurial vision, which manifests itself in the mission (actually the *mission statement*). This applies not only to private enterprises but also to the public sector, to organizations, foundations, and to associations. By the way, the statement that a BPR project is doomed for failure when it is not based on a clearly formulated and openly communicated mission is also valid. The mission of an organization should reflect the "vocation" of the organization, what purpose it serves, the responsible persons standing behind it, which customers are being supplied with what products and services, and what benefits arise for the customer from this. Increasingly important are also statements about what responsibility the enterprise will assume for its customers and business partners, its staff, and ultimately for society and the environment.

Business process reengineering focuses on creating a system of networked business processes, using these effectively to support organizational regulations and information system technologies to optimally fulfill an organization's mission. Optimality is defined not only on the basis of operational parameters, such as costs, product and service quality, or even market shares but also consciously on values that reflect the benefits to the individual, the society, and the environment. Since organizations ordinarily do not represent a closed system, all relevant external influence factors must invariably be taken into account in connection with BPR, as clearly illustrated in Fig. 5.2.

In the center of this figure, we find the rough procedure of the BPR: Business objectives are defined, beginning with the mission that is suitable to measure the success of the mission implementation. Mission and goals then generate a frame in which strategies are developed and implemented by business processes and

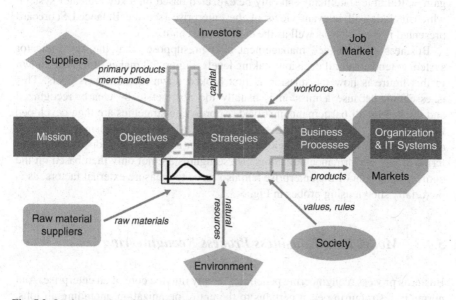

Fig. 5.2 Implementation of the corporate mission

supporting IT systems and organizational regulations as well. From the figure, it is obvious that a variety of external factors must be taken into account with each enterprise consideration, in which meanwhile a global context can be premised for a majority of the enterprises. Both risks and opportunities arise from the external factors, and experience shows that these are often inextricably linked. BPR processes must pay particular attention to this integration for the optimal exploitation of success potentials.

5.1.2   Business Performance Management

The leading economies of the world were marked by sustained growth after World War II—with moderate cyclic fluctuations. Long-term prognoses were possible in this "predictable" economic environment, as well as the strategically planned opening of markets. The increasing globalization of emerging and collapsing economies, economic and environmental crises, threats to health and safety, and a rapid change in values—in connection with the media flood—have fundamentally changed the rules in the private and public sectors. Entirely new forms of corporate governance are called for that combine *sustainability* with responsiveness as well a consistent pursuit of the corporate mission. Elastic business processes and an effective business performance management have proven to be factors for success.

Business performance management refers to the entire process of corporate governance based on key performance indicators. It therefore includes the definition of a key indicator system as well as its implementation, ongoing monitoring with evaluation of the indicators, and the control of the enterprise as a result of knowledge gained. Reliable statements can only be expected based on a key indicator system, which includes all relevant views of the enterprise (see the Balanced Scorecard presented in Sect. 4.1) as well as the entire value chain.

Business performance management also presupposes that the key indicator system extends over all decision-making levels. Figure 5.3 makes this clear. Shown in this figure is how the mission is first broken down into business goals. This is essential, because a mission is usually too abstract to be clearly recognized and tracked by all participants involved. Appropriate strategies are then developed to achieve the business objectives (see Chap. 4). To make business objective achievement and success strategies measurable, it is necessary to operationalize in terms of key performance indicators. These figures are not only then based on the entire value chain of the enterprise but also serve to measure external factors, as is pictorially shown using probes in Fig. 5.3.

5.1.3   Model-Based Business Process Reengineering

Business process reengineering penetrates deeply into the core of an enterprise. And normally restructuring even pertains to the entire organization, including all jobs,

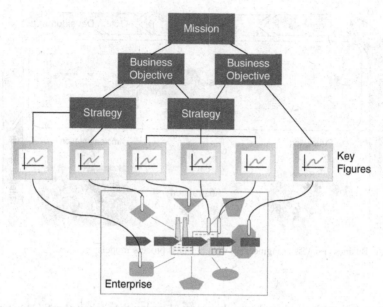

Fig. 5.3 Operationalization of objectives and strategies

workflows, and business rules. In this respect, BPR affects all parties involved in the business process execution: all employees over all hierarchical levels, customers and business partners, and of course the owners as well. Moreover, exactly this fact makes BPR so difficult, preventing the compilation of a generally applicable BPR procedure model. Nevertheless, some useful approaches have emerged in practice; their description, however, would go far beyond the scope of this book. However, it is important to understand the significance of business process models for BPR. For this purpose, a process concept for model-based BPR is outlined in Fig. 5.4.

The process is roughly divided into the phases of *diagnosis*, *analysis*, *option development*, and *implementation*. Diagnosis deals with an examination of existing business processes, whereas the level of detail of the "as-is examination" very much depends on the meaning attached to previous processes as well as which insights can be expected from the examination of the strengths and weaknesses. Guided by the company mission, an analysis phase takes place to define the business model, the establishment of the target system, as well as an elaboration of specific business strategies. In general, this also results in a business process architecture that is very general at this point. All this defines an organizational frame in which different options are then developed. Those include a system of business processes where the focus always lies on the core business processes. Support and enterprise management processes are considered only in transition to implementation, that is, when a (pre-) decision to implement the option has already been made. During

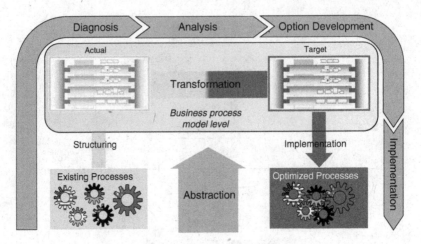

Fig. 5.4 Business process reengineering with business process models

implementation, the conversion of the selected option then takes place. Once again, emphasis should be placed on the importance of change management at this point, which in practice often makes a phased implementation of the redesigned business processes necessary.

With BPR projects, an intensive use of conventional organizational materials, techniques, and methods (flip chart, pin board, questionnaires, etc.) has proven effective. These reach their limits, however, when it comes to a discussion of specific business processes, business objects, or rules. Misunderstandings then occur, and unrecognized inconsistencies and incomplete statements impede informal communications considerably, often leading to questionable results. Also with respect to documentation, significant quality deficiencies can be observed. Working with business process models can help here, especially when appropriate software tools are available.

Besides these obvious advantages, a model use in BPR projects has another problem, which must be addressed and which is often underestimated, albeit it sometimes leads the BPR efforts in practice to downright absurdity. The problem is that the user finds it extremely difficult to let go of his "old, retracted" processes. New process ideas or even process innovations cannot be expected in such cases. Only an abstraction will help in this case. It must make a discussion at the level of genuine business requirements possible—without throwing unused essential knowledge and experience overboard. Business process models are the drug of choice here! They abstract from the details of specifically implemented business processes, allowing a rapid development and evaluation of various process alternatives at a technical level. The significance of the models for the quality of communication and documentation has already been pointed out in many places in this book.

5.1.4 Use of Reference Models

When working with business process models, solutions are produced that prove themselves repeatedly, therefore making them candidates for reuse in future projects. However, such models must be generalized and quality-assured prior to reuse. Renowned consulting firms achieve substantial competitive advantages with such "best practice models" or "knowledge bases." In many cases, the manufacturers of business process tools also offer such models.

Best practice models are frequently used even in BPR projects. However, they pose a danger in that they obscure the focus on completely new solution variants. For this reason, the use of reference models is recommended, especially in the preparation of details, but not in the preparation of initial process ideas.

Reference models for BPR must ideally be oriented toward a specific industry or adapted to a specific area of application, so that they create a conceptual framework for all project participants based on its conceptuality. And the models, within their scope, must be sharply generalized so as not to constrain their use. With eTOM and SCOR, we mention two widely used reference models at this point, which provide good services in worldwide BPR projects.

5.1.4.1 eTOM® Business Process Framework

The *TeleManagement Forum* is an international consortium of communications service providers and their suppliers. In the context of the *enhanced Telecom Operations Map®* initiative (eTOM® for short), the TeleManagement Forum supports service providers in the telecommunications industry and their business partners with a comprehensive business process framework. Based on an overall presentation of the value chain, eTOM describes in a generic form all business processes of a communication service provider, listing them according to their importance and priority. The processes are divided into three areas: *Strategy, Infrastructure and Product, Enterprise Management and Operations*. eTOM serves primarily not only as a reference model for service providers in business process reengineering projects but also as a neutral reference point for partnering models, alliances, and agreements with other providers and suppliers.

5.1.4.2 SCOR® Supply Chain Operations Reference Model

Supply chains characterize themselves (not only in industrial environments) through the integration of different business partners that are in many cases scattered across the globe. Supply chains are therefore naturally collaborative processes whose design ideally includes all process partners involved. This requires a uniform and easily understandable communication platform. With SCOR, the *Supply Chain Council* offers a proven process reference model for this. The aim of the model is to provide users with a tool which will enable them to discuss, reengineer, and optimize supply chain management processes within the enterprise and with business partners.

5.2 Business Process Management and SOA

Since the mid-1990s, business processes have always become the center of debate when it comes to corporate strategy and organizational issues. Even with the introduction of packaged business application software (such as SAP or Oracle Applications), the use of business process models has long been state of the art (see Sect. 5.3). In the individual development of information systems, however, its significance has always been underestimated. Many projects that failed due to imprecise or lack of process definitions prove the accuracy of this statement.

With the increasing use of the service-oriented architecture (SOA) concept, business processes have now gained an entirely new meaning. First, SOA applications have already shown that an efficient infrastructure for process-based management and execution of Web services and applications alone is no solution. A consistent design of the business processes that make up the heart of an SOA, in accordance with the requirements of the departments, is more important. Only when the processes really meet the business requirements can their automation provide the best results. Based on these considerations, holistic business process management, which has already been presented in Sect. 2.5, has long surpassed the topic of SOA in its significance. And it is undisputed that a consideration of business processes now belongs at the center of each strategy, organization, and IT project. Business process models then act as a central reference point for all technical specifications and build the bridge to the specific implementation in the form of organizational and IT solutions.

5.2.1 Interactions Between Business and IT

The increasing proliferation of SOA is driven by requirements from the business field. IT must respond to new business strategies that are trimmed to modification and are quickly adaptable to future developments at any time. Corporate management rightly demands business process solutions and information system platforms that allow a quick and economic implementation of such strategies. Invariably, part of the implementation is a seamless integration of applications and Web services along the supply chain. How can the requisite flexibility of the integration be achieved without a drastic increase in project costs? How can the heterogeneity of applications and services be taken into account, and how can existing investments be secured to the application environment? A SOA will provide the answer to these questions in the context of a holistic business process management.

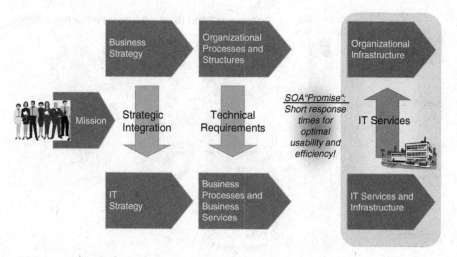

Fig. 5.5 Interactions between business and IT

Figure 5.5 summarizes these considerations in a diagram. Based on a company's mission, strategic considerations are made which eventually result in organizational processes and structures that will be implemented into a suitable infrastructure. Shown are the interactions that business-driven activities have on the IT. IT strategy is deduced from the business strategy, taking into account the current state of information and communication technology. Building on this, business processes and business services—in the context of organizational concepts—will be developed based on service-oriented IT infrastructure and implemented IT services (Web services and applications) and are then made available to the business department as IT services. The SOA "promise" to the specialized areas is then to provide fast response times to new business requirements with optimum usability and efficiency.

5.2.2 Model-Driven Implementation of an SOA

There is no generally accepted definition for SOA. For this reason, in practice, system architectures that are built up completely different are described as a SOA. Frankly, we do not lend any great significance to this term; instead, we see this as holistic business process management. Ideally, this would include an implementation in the form of Web services and application components that are orchestrated into largely automated processes wherever possible. In Fig. 5.6, an example of an SOA is shown which has been implemented by a company in the electronics industry. The enterprise serves both business and private customers. For this purpose, target group-oriented Web portals (business-to-business/B2B and business-to-consumer/B2C) are available, each even including an e-Store functionality.

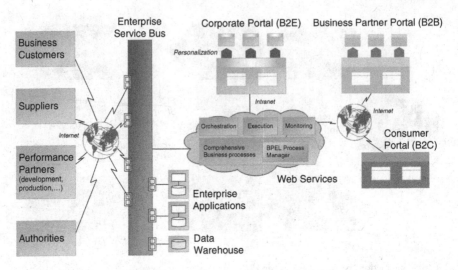

Fig. 5.6 Sample structure of a SOA

The basis of the represented SOA forms an *Enterprise Service Bus* (ESB), which is responsible for integration at the data level. It offers an open, adaptable integration platform, which supports different technologies and protocols for the linking of the various systems. Message exchange takes place either synchronously or asynchronously. Features include extensive mechanisms for the transformation of data through XSLT and for the semantic mapping of business objects between systems. The ESB also takes over the safe routing of data between source and target systems.

In this example, the Internet linking of external process partners, as well as that of the business applications and data warehouses, is implemented directly via the ESB. The Internet portals and intranet-based corporate portal (business-to-employee/B2E), through which the company's employees receive important business assessment, collaboration, and knowledge management, are integrated by BPEL processes. This concept has the advantage that in BPEL processes, the complete process logic can be deposited in a flexible manner and then be evaluated at execution time. Sophisticated monitoring capabilities enable an ongoing process improvement on the basis of key process indicators.

Processes are included not only in the BPEL processes but also in the routing of ESB data packets and the proffered user functions. All components of the SOA can fulfill the technical requirements only if they are suited to the business processes concerned. This once again underlines the importance of holistic business process management: Models form the backbone of any professionally designed SOA solution. In an easily understood graphic form, models represent the blueprint of the SOA in that they describe the underlying business processes and business services (see Sect. 5.3). By abstraction of the details of the technical implementation, they provide transparency and are the most important communication medium when it comes to business issues. Thus, for the first time, emancipated decision makers and business experts, who can formulate their requirements clearly and vividly, accompany the IT specialist. The results are well-documented business processes, which form a solid foundation for implementation in an SOA, thereby achieving a high level of acceptance in daily use.

5.2.3 Best Practices and Reference Models for SOA

The close cooperation between business and IT, as part of an SOA, makes the use of business process models, represented by successive detailing on the IT-based implementation, inevitable. Furthermore, reference models can accelerate the implementation decisively with predefined business processes and hierarchies. The design of such models must therefore transpire in layers of different granularity, as previously described in Chap. 4 under best practice and reference models. With such hierarchical models, business processes can be comprehensively described based on an SOA, from the broad procedures to detailed functions, meaning the various implementation services (in this example, Web services) will be described with a formal model.

XML nets are used at all levels in the modeling of the procedures in the business processes. Ambiguous processes and function descriptions are avoided through the use of a formal language. Service-oriented structuring, based on encapsulated services, provides transparency regarding the underlying IT systems. In business process models, the concepts of a SOA is considered so that an orchestration of complex processes of existing services will be made possible at different levels. To manage the complexity, a multilayered process hierarchy is established together with the four layers illustrated in Sect. 4.6. This depth of detail has clearly proven itself in practical projects. The quantity is adjusted accordingly, depending on the size of the project. The process descriptions originate from business processes at higher levels of abstraction, specifying these in lower detail layers with existing or yet to be realized implementation services.

At the highest level—the *basic business service orchestration*—basic business services can be orchestrated to enterprise-wide and overlapping process maps. A basic business service orchestration is the compilation of several basic business services for mapping the core processes in an enterprise.

The single basic business services are represented as refinements in a broad procedure in the process overview. The individual steps then represent the process components that need to be performed, for example, for the approval of an offer. The use of significant and general business terms in the naming of the steps show the still high level of abstraction in this layer.

Beneath the process overview, the detailed procedures of the individual process components, in most cases two layers, are described in further detail. From here, the level begins, that is, to be implemented on the basis of tangible technical implementation services. Here, roles are already assigned to all activities that are relevant to the execution of processes. Activities to be carried out automatically, for example, will be assigned with the role System. The activities here are assigned to particular implementation services that are to be carried out in each case. With the assignment of activity to implementation service, the respective use of the service is described in the context of the process. Ideally, the implementation services already exist and can be assigned from the enterprise's service library. Alternatively, new implementation services can be defined that still have to be put into effect.

Figure 5.7 shows the implementation of these levels of detail with XML nets. These can then be transformed with special algorithms into BPEL, based on enrichment with additional information about the underlying technical web services, so that the modeled business processes can be carried out in an SOA. In such extended XML nets, there must be exactly one object store without an incoming edge. This object store represents the *input* for the XML net. Similarly, there is exactly one object store that does not have an outgoing edge. This object store then simultaneously represents the network *output*. The XML Schema definitions of the input and output object store specify which messages of the BPEL process are to be expected at the beginning and what to send in the end, respectively. XML Schema definitions of the object store in pre- and post-areas of activities, that lie between input and output object store, see themselves as the schemas of those messages that are sent to an appropriate Web service or return to the BPEL process. The additionally required data, in comparison to pure XML nets that must be stored for the transformation to BPEL, is assigned to activities. If a Web service is to be connected to an activity, then the WSDL file must be available and be correspondingly assigned. The *Web Service Description Language* (WSDL) is

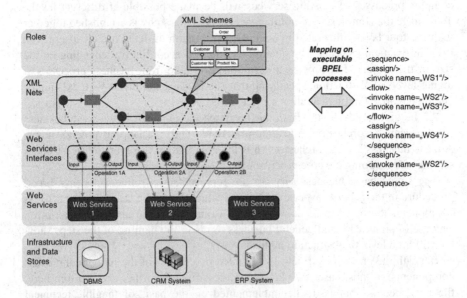

Fig. 5.7 Technical implementation of XML nets in an SOA

used for a platform-independent description of services in an SOA based on Web Services. WSDL is an XML-based language for describing Web services and their interfaces. In the description of a Web service, its functionality and information concerning its invocation and use must be given. On the basis of a WSDL file, further activity attributes such as, for example, the selection of the corresponding Web service operation for the current process step, must be selected. Moreover, the type of corresponding base activity must be established. It indicates which BPEL-based activity will represent this transition. Receive, reply, invoke, empty, and wait activities can be specified.

For the execution of processes, full integration architectures such as the *Oracle Application Integration Architecture* (Oracle AIA) can be employed using BPEL as a process execution technology. By virtue of the fundamental, technically detached description of the processes with Petri or XML nets, the process descriptions can also generate algorithms for other execution technologies, taking the technical aspects into account.

5.3 Process-Oriented Introduction of Business Software

Increasingly, the introduction of configurable business software, such as SAP, Oracle Applications, or Microsoft Dynamics, already makes use of SOA concepts and technologies. Model-driven approaches to defining and implementing such software systems are henceforth called for. The concept of an abstract implementation of business processes based on business services realized in the Horus method (see Sect. 4.5) is particularly suitable for this purpose. In addition, reference models with predefined business processes, as provided for in the Horus method, expedite the implementation of standard software decisively, thereby substantially improving the quality of results achieved.

5.3.1 Why the Introduction of a Business Software Is Difficult

There are numerous reports of failed or at least severely delayed and costly software projects. Many of these projects deal with the introduction of standard software, albeit this at first appears easier than developing new custom software. Why business software projects appear to be more difficult will be explained below, in order to derive from it an improved introduction process.

It is often discovered only during the course of the implementation of business software that the business processes of the standard software at hand do not correspond to the current processes in the enterprise. The comprehensive functionality of a standard software and the resulting complexity lead to a divergent understanding of the term "standard" with respect to these processes. Heterogeneous IT system landscapes are another reason for problems in the introduction of standard software.

Complex interface solutions for the integration of different systems require time and expenses. Regarding the costs of introduction, it is—often wrongly—expected that standard software is significantly cheaper than a comparable individual development. For this purpose, standard software usually offers the possibility of building the desired software solution from modules for different areas, which can also be purchased separately. This, in turn, increases demands on the flexibility of the implementation process.

With the introduction of business software, large parts of an enterprise will generally be affected, as the business processes provided by the software are cross-departmental in most cases. Standard software provides extensive features and predefined business processes, which cannot be customized randomly, but only within the framework predetermined by the software itself. A lack of transparency of the functionality of standard software based on the complexity on the one side, and unclear requirements on behalf of the departments that are to use the systems later, pose problems in the introduction. Unclear requirements often result from a missing or inaccurate, that is, informally established business process and function definition. Even if the processes have already been defined in advance with their detailed requirements, a direct or possibly even automatic mapping onto the processes and functions of the standard software under consideration is difficult. The reasons for this are the conceptual and methodical differences between the tools and procedures used in line with the analysis and documentation of the processes implemented within the standard software.

For business users, introducing a new business software is always a challenge, as entirely different skills are required than those needed in daily business, and secondly, the project work is often done in addition to the daily standard tasks. The induction into new business software is difficult because of the complexity of the software and the documentation is correspondingly large. Furthermore, the true benefit of such solutions is often visible only with the interplay realized by the software from several areas of an enterprise. This overlapping view of the solution remains hidden for many users at first. This problem is also often found in the system documentation, as this is geared purely functional and not process-oriented. The points listed result in long project execution times and often result in budget overruns. Furthermore, functions not covered by the standard software are often only identified during system testing.

5.3.2 Model-Driven, Service-Oriented Implementation Approach

Many of the described problems cannot be remedied with traditional business software introduction methods and are therefore demanding novel approaches. So far, the introduction of business software has taken place in the context of traditional software engineering, starting from a requirements analysis up to the go live and operation of the system. The modeling of business processes to be implemented as part of the requirements analysis provides the basis for the design and architecture of the system. A problem with this approach to the introduction of standard software is the deviation of the company-specific business processes from the prescribed processes of standard application software. The approach of a multilayer model will allow for a degree of abstraction-based representation of business services, that is, the functionality of the business software at different levels. Business process models in conjunction with business service models, as provided by the Horus method, reduce complexity and enable flexible business process management through the orchestration of business services. These can be combined horizontally with comprehensive business processes, linking them to one another vertically through refinements. An implementation of these processes can take place based on the BPEL standard (see Sect. 5.2), which is already being used in many business software products for system integration.

An approach for the introduction of business software designed on the basis of the Horus method uses reference models as a key technology. Reference models that describe the business services of standard software must then be constructed in such a manner so that they provide documentation aligned to the business processes of the business software. This means that the reference models must base on the fundamental processes that can be configured with the appropriate modules of the standard software. Furthermore, the user must be led to detailed processes from rough general business management processes in a top down approach that describes the specific use of the business software up to the functional level. In this structuring, general business terms should be semantically transferred to the upper concept levels in the detailed processes of the business software. Ambiguous process and function descriptions can be avoided by using a formal model.

The informal requirements of departments, if any, should be assigned to the process models in the appropriate places to examine the coverage ratio of the standard software at an early stage. A service-oriented structuring of the business software based on encapsulated business services provides transparency regarding the horizontal and vertical relationships within the software and especially the integration with other systems. The process models should take into account the standards of a SOA, that is, consider the standards of Web services so that an orchestration of complex processes from existing services is allowed at different levels. If BPEL is used for the realization of general processes, then this should be ready to be generated from the process models. The aim is to assemble a system based on standard software modules and to realize model-driven integration solutions based on business processes.

5.3.3 Practical Use of a Business Service Reference Model

The proposed implementation approach requires the provision of reference models which meet the requirements of the Horus method described in Sect. 4.6. The following describes a sample section of a business service reference model which

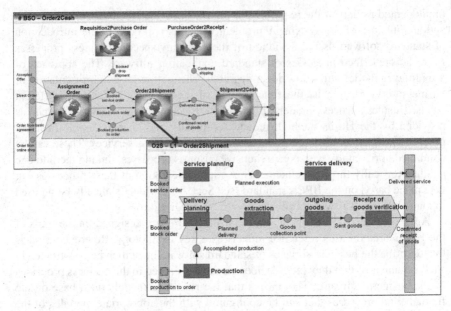

Fig. 5.8 Levels 0 (*top*) und 1 (*bottom*) of the Order2Cash business service

defines a composite business service Order2Cash.[1] An implementation of this service using Oracle Applications—in this case, the Oracle E-Business Suite (in short: EBS)—has already been realized in several projects based on the Oracle modules Order Management, Accounts Receivable, Cash Management, and General Ledger.

The orchestrated Level 0 process shown in Fig. 5.8 depicts the interaction of various business services for the Order2Cash process. The core process describes the procedure of a commission right up to the inpayment of the appropriate order. The orchestrated process already includes business services from the purchasing side, as these are needed for orders that are to be processed as third party transactions. The Oracle modules *i*Procurement, Purchasing, and Accounts Payable are also required in this instance.

The depiction of the Level 1 process in Fig. 5.8 shows the broad process within basic business service Order2Shipment. The steps shown in the broad procedure are process components that are required for the delivery of an order. The use of significant and general business terms in the naming of the steps indicate the high level of abstraction in this layer. The various procedures are already considered here, however, depending on the transaction account, that is, service orders, stock orders, and production orders are treated differently.

---

[1]Extract from a reference model which is available as Horus Knowledge Base™, a product of Horus software GmbH, Ettlingen, Germany.

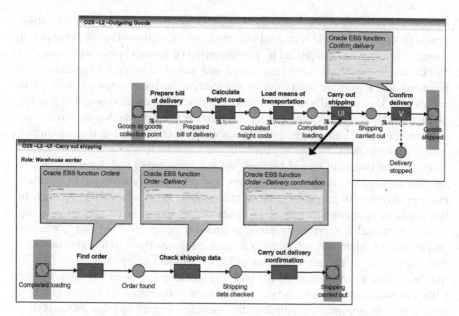

Fig. 5.9 Detail process `Outgoing Goods` and user instruction `Carry out shipping`

The top of Fig. 5.9 shows the detailed procedure within process component `Shipping` of business service `Order2Shipment`. When compared to the reference model design in Sect. 4.6.2, it is obvious that Level 2 has been omitted in this particular model. Every activity has already been assigned a role here. For example, the packing list is created by the warehouse workers, but the final confirmation of delivery is made by the warehouse manager. Activities to be carried out automatically, for example, will be assigned to role `System`. In addition, individual EBS functions (services) can be assigned to the activities here. With the assignment between activity and function, the respective use will be described in the context of the process. Alternatively, new functions can be defined which are then also to be realized within the context of the implementation.

The lower part of Fig. 5.9 shows the user instructions for `Carry out shipping`. The execution of shipping, using the corresponding Oracle EBS function, is defined here for role `Warehouse worker`. Individual EBS functions can be additionally defined for the activities here as well, in this case the instruction steps, if they are not available already.

5.3.4   Migration of a Business Software

In the previous descriptions for the use of model-driven processes in business software projects, the introduction of this software from scratch was tacitly assumed.

As business software is often used for a period of more than 10 years, an additional important application field is opened with the implementation of release changes. If a release change is accompanied by reengineering of business processes supported by business software—this can be assumed with so-called major release changes— the need for a genuine migration of the current business software solution is mandatory. This is usually accompanied by a functional expansion and upgrading of basic technologies. A report from a migration project which was carried out at a medium-sized supply enterprise (trade and manufacturing) in the automotive industry follows next.

During the course of its use, business software develops a high level of maturity through adaptations, further development, and rehearsed procedures. In contrast, changes in business processes make a realignment of the software necessary. In this field, an upcoming migration of business software may be viewed not only from a technical but primarily from a business perspective. In this particular project, this problem was solved by placing a careful analysis to improve business processes prior to the migration, in order to provide an optimal basis for the introduction of a new release of the business software used—in this case, Oracle EBS. The standard software has successfully been in operation for numerous years, with some customizations, including the modules `Purchasing`, `Inventory Management`, and `Order Management`. The standard software is seamlessly embedded into a heterogeneous system landscape.

The greatest optimization potential was identified in the procurement process prior to the migration. As a first step, a reengineering project for the cross-sector procurement process was established. This process affects not only the actual purchase but also the areas of order acceptance, item setup, supplier administration, and auditing.

Below is a report of experiences in business process reengineering and the expected effects in the subsequent migration. At the forefront is the approach of the as-is analysis, right through to the definition of optimal processes as a target for the migration of business software.

5.3.4.1   As-Is Analysis

The project started with an analysis of existing business processes. The as-is situation, in the form of a hierarchically structured process model, was initially included. The process hierarchy consisted of five levels: context model, business process architecture model, and below this a detailing of core process `Procurement` laid out over three levels. Figure 5.10 shows the procurement process at a glance.

During the documentation of the actual state, the current vulnerabilities were deposited into the models as details. Graphically, this is identified by gray activities in the current processes. Furthermore, textual descriptions of the problems are deposited at the corresponding steps of the processes. No problems arise with the dark activities of the process in the as-is state. Problems are stored with the gray steps, or there are problems in the underlying detail processes. For example, it can be

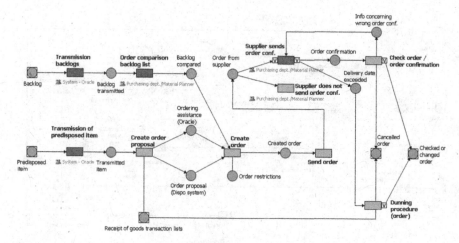

Fig. 5.10 The procurement process as is (Level 1)

noted with the as-is Procurement process that there is no procedurally specified approach and no IT-based implementation in the event that a supplier does not send an order confirmation; this is dealt with in the actual state only at transgression of the delivery date. By assigning roles, it became apparent that responsibilities for some process steps in the current processes were not clearly defined. The result of the actual-state analysis was a documentation of the current processes across all five process layers, recording all problems and open points within the examined area. The process hierarchy was then set as the basis for the subsequent to-be analysis.

5.3.4.2 To-Be Analysis

A target model was designed based on the developed process structure, the documented problems, and open points of the as-is state analysis. The processes were improved based on the discussions of the respectively responsible employees. Detail processes were discussed internally and improved within departments, while the overall interaction of the areas was discussed and improved in a wider context. Figure 5.11 shows the optimized core process Procurement, where all requirements from the as-is model have been fulfilled. On the one hand, these consist of a specific process with clear responsibilities for certain, previously obscure subprocesses or steps. On the other hand, requests directed toward an IT implementation have been deposited at the detail level, which should be realized in the migration to a new release of Oracle E-Business Suite by appropriate configuration of the available standard functionality, by setting up specific workflows or additional functionalities.

The proposals made by each work group were discussed mutually in large project workshops to come to an optimized overall process. The jointly developed central result is a target business process model that represents the cross-functional

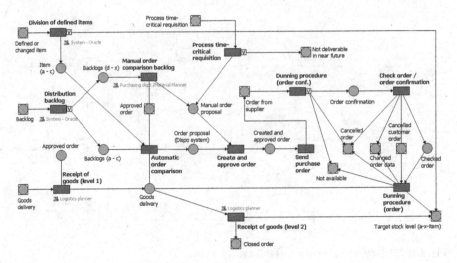

Fig. 5.11 To-be procurement process (Level 1)

optimized procurement process, from a customer inquiry or an order from the Web shop up to the closed order or the achievable target stock level of items, pinpointing the interfaces between the areas and thus defining the accountabilities. As a final result, a plan of action was created from the target model based on the cumulated future adjustments and improvements. On the one hand, the action plan contains IT-related software components or adjustments that are to be implemented. On the other hand, purely organizational measures are included which do not entail any IT-related changes but improve the business process in itself. These were partially implemented before the subsequent migration and thus enabled a measurable success pretty soon.

5.3.4.3 Conclusion

The practical project presented here could prove that a reengineering for the improvement of business processes done prior to the migration of a new business software release provides valuable results. The problems are accurately recorded at the sites of their occurrence through model-based documentation and can therefore be successively edited in the target model. This will counteract the danger of forgetting important points in the migration or the porting of errors. Not to be underestimated is the fact that a solution is formed through the jointly developed model, which focuses on the enterprise requirements, supported by all parties involved. The result is a common vision with common goals for all parties involved, both for the departmental areas as well as IT.

The use of process models as part of reengineering ensures, across different tiers, that each process can be easily integrated into the entire enterprise procedure. Complex interactions become manageable. This creates a reliable basis for the subsequent migration. This can ideally be carried out on the exact specifications of the formal model. The requirements for new standard functionalities can be tested, or they serve as an implementation specification for workflow and additional developments. A main advantage of this approach is that the IT-related requirements result from the optimized business process; that is unnecessary developments are minimized. In addition, improvements based on organizational changes can be achieved in the forefront of the migration, which has a positive impact on the return on investment for the migration.

5.4   Governance, Risk and Compliance

The days where an enterprise could be led entirely in an autocratic "lord of the manor" fashion are long gone. Regulators respond with increasingly complex regulations to the global escalation of economic, environmental, and computer crimes. The crux here is that for a globally active enterprise, it no longer suffices to consider only the national regulations at the enterprise level, but rather all regulations must be considered which are affected in the context of transnational business processes. These regulations are not even compatible in many cases. To this end, investors and financial institutions demand an effective risk management system, for example, through the establishment of early warning systems to identify risks and to create greater transparency in financial processes. The keywords here are SOX[2] and Basel II[3]. Furthermore, increasingly shorter half-life strategic decisions can only be met with efficiently managed and secure business processes. In short: *Governance*, *risk*, and *compliance* issues (GRC for short) are at the top of the management's agenda; these topics define one of the most important application areas for business process engineering. The benefits of comprehensive business process models with GRC are particularly greater in number, because most of the requirements relate to the quality of process control and transparency of business operations. But first a short disambiguation:

- *Governance* is running a business on the basis of clearly understood and formulated business objectives and instructions. Important conditions are legal compliance and completeness. Governance thus extends across all business units and levels, which is why we speak of *horizontal* and *vertical* governance.
- *Risk management* is the collection of all measures for dealing with known and unknown enterprise-internal as well as enterprise-external risks. These include the establishment of early warning systems to identify risks as well as measures to eliminate potential risks and for the treatment of incurred risks.

---

[2]The Sarbanes-Oxley Act (SOX) is a US federal law that ensures the accuracy and reliability of financial data published by enterprises.

[3]Basel II designates the collectivity of capital regulations compiled by the Basel Committee on Banking Supervision. These regulations are mandatory in the EU states, in the context of the extension of credit and credit trade, for all financial service providers since 2007.

- *Compliance* denotes conforming to a rule, correspondence, or conformity with a specification, policy, standard, or law with (ethical and moral) principles and procedures, including standards (e.g., ISO) and clearly defined conventions. Compliance fulfillment can be both enforced (e.g., by law) or voluntary (e.g., adherence to standards).

5.4.1 Influencing Factors and GRC Mechanisms

In corporate practice, it has been proven to treat governance, risk, and compliance management in a cross-thematic context. The reasons are obvious: Very many interdependencies exist; synergies arise during implementation that on the one hand enhance the effectiveness of planned actions, contributing to cost reductions on the other. By the way, companies that see GRC not primarily as a burden, but above all as an opportunity to improve business processes, achieve genuine cost savings and improve their competitive positions.

Figure 5.12 shows the typical structure of a GRC approach. The number of external requirements seems overwhelming for the observance of and compliance with corporate records management, in many cases setting forth personal liability. Their task is to formulate appropriate instructions, to communicate, and to monitor their compliance. Even more: The directives should be complete, efficient, and effective, therefore consistent in themselves. It is also necessary to implement mechanisms that monitor and control the execution of the directives. In addition,

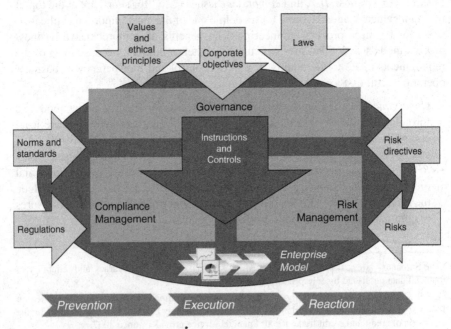

Fig. 5.12 Influencing factors and GRC mechanisms

reactive mechanisms are to be provided for, ensuring that the enterprise immediately takes proper measures, in the case of imminent or an actual violation of regulations, to limit damage to the periphery as well as the enterprise itself. Responsible enterprises pay the highest attention to preventive mechanisms. With the avoidance of risks and compliance violations lies the key to significant cost savings and prudent market trade, often resulting in interesting competitive advantages.

However, it is clear from these considerations that the drafting and subsequent implementation of a comprehensive GRC approach bears a high degree of complexity. This is actually manageable only if the enterprise connections are represented in a consistent model. Analysis and optimization are possible based on this model, as well as development of an effective GRC system. In this respect, GRC is one of the most important fields of application of the Horus method and Horus tools.

5.4.2 Implementation of GRC in an Organizational Context

Prior to the introduction of GRC into an enterprise, it is often debated whether it is a business project or an IT project. "Both" is the correct answer here. A look at Fig. 5.13 illustrates this. GRC always lies in the responsibility of the enterprise management, therefore remaining a strategic project. GRC also digs deep into the enterprise, penetrating it by implementing mechanisms that work at all levels— from the strategy to business processes and application software, right up to the IT platform.

Set forth from the multitude of mechanisms, it is advisable to understand GRC not as a simple project but as a strategic program in which several time-coordinated projects are implemented. It is also important to understand that GRC is not only a "concern of the finance department," as one often encounters within an enterprise. GRC in fact encompasses all business processes and organizational units of the enterprise, consciously involving the collaboration with customers and business partners of all kinds. The resulting complexity can only be mastered with business models.

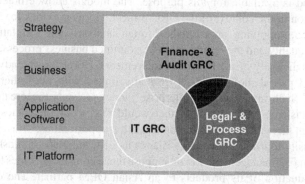

Fig. 5.13 Embedding of GRC within a corporate context

GRC is often structured into three packages of measures that reflect different views of GRC but which are closely related to one other:

- *Finance and Audit GRC.* SOX, Basel II, country-specific principles of proper accounting, etc., are the drivers in finance and audit GRC. A close cooperation between the auditors and the financial and tax authorities is a requirement. Internal control systems are to ensure the correct and compliant implementation of the processes in finance and accounting. Of particular significance are the monitoring of business transactions, based on corporate performance indicators (key performance indicator, KPI) and risks (key risk indicator, KRI).
- *Legal and Process GRC.* Legal and process GRC places the operative business in the center of consideration. Are all legal requirements fulfilled? Customs and tax issues will be resolved. Moreover, do the business processes guarantee the satisfaction of norms (e.g., ISO, DIN) and standards (including industry standards) across national borders? Market risks and endangerment through a business interruption (e.g., force majeure) must also be taken into account.
- *IT GRC.* Information technology (IT) not only plays an important role in GRC with the implementation of the GRC mechanisms—think of the automation of business processes and monitoring of key indicators—but also holds significant risk potentials. In addition, IT is subject to numerous regulations, such as with data protection (e.g., Federal Data Protection Act). An appropriate course of action guarantees a secure and legally compliant use of all information resources. In addition, programmatic anomalies and violations of existing regulations must be avoided, for example, regarding the segregation of duties (SoD).

5.4.3 Prevention of Information Islands

The implementation of GRC projects has an intrinsic complexity, which results from the large number of fields of action as well as from the diversity of business requirements. This complexity is manageable only if easy-to-understand enterprise models are used, and a systematic procedure for creating these models exists. The Horus method is available for this purpose. The models allow efficient forms of communication in the context of the GRC project. Horus provides for a consistent documentation, supplying approaches through analysis and simulation for the assurance of quality and the optimization of examined business processes.

As for the diversity of the business requirements, Horus has the advantage that the generated partial models can be formally linked with one other, as shown in Fig. 5.14. Such an integrated enterprise model prevents the creation of new "information islands" through GRC that would lead to inefficiencies and hence would stand in the way of interesting optimization opportunities.

The necessity to avoid information islands in GRC solutions is illustrated by an example from risk management. Let us suppose that a company decides to outsource the final production of its products to an Asian OEM partner. The company is prepared to assume transportation risks with delivery to its strategic end customers

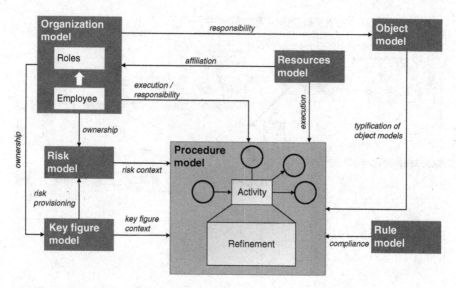

Fig. 5.14 Integrated Horus Enterprise model

in the European market. To avoid transport risks, preventive action is taken (e.g., increase in stocks): Real-time monitoring of transports by means of a sophisticated key indicator system will be established, and it will be clearly regulated (by reactive measures) what will happen if delays do occur in the delivery to the end customer (such as an early warning system or delivery from local stock). The enterprise has now done everything correctly when viewed from an isolated risk assessment point of view. However, this is not sufficient. Rather, it is necessary to consider what it will cost the enterprise to assume this risk in transportation; the value proposition incurred by OEM manufacturing in Asia is then to be compared to these costs. Not infrequently, such a risk-value-cost analysis leads to the OEM process variant being discarded, replacing this with an in-house or near-shore production.

This example once again highlights the benefits of working with formal enterprise models. Figure 5.15 shows an extract example of a model which was used within the scope of a finance and audit GRC project. It was created based on a Horus Business Services Knowledge Base. Shown are accounting procedures, especially the aligning of the general ledger and the integration of the alignment into the end-of-month settlement.

5.5 Managed Services and ITIL

Public and private enterprises in all industries today feel an unprecedented competition and cost pressure. Globalization, virtualization, and transparency are the challenges that enterprises must face. A look at prevailing practice shows that

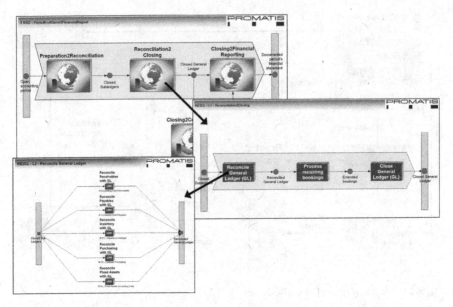

Fig. 5.15 Business service model from a finance and audit GRC project

successful enterprises often distinguish themselves through intelligent, adaptive business processes and a perfectly matched information technology. In view of the constant changes that enterprises are exposed to, they must make great efforts to secure their success in the longer term. How can processes and technologies quickly adapt to changing requirements? How and when are which innovations to be implemented? How will the increasing complexity of the systems be taken into account? How can predetermined service levels be met, such as scalability, high availability as well as security be guaranteed? These are all questions that need answers.

5.5.1 Outsourcing vs. Managed Services

Many companies respond with outsourcing strategies to these issues, which may range from an outsourcing of infrastructure to an outsourcing of complete application landscapes. However, complex and long-term outsourcing contracts often limit an enterprise's ability to react to new challenges in an unreasonable manner. Many outsourcing customers have bitterly regretted relinquishing responsibility for personnel, infrastructure, and operational IT goals in hindsight, at the latest when they, under great effort, had to make their way back through insourcing. An elegant alternative is provided by *managed services* that ultimately represent a special form of outsourcing: Responsibility remains with the client, who then passes parts of it on to a service partner for a limited time, according to his wishes and desires. In this way, the customer can concentrate on his core competencies, gaining additional capacities, special expertise, and access to new technologies according to his or her current efficiency. This leads to improved responsiveness to changing business needs and a higher level of service—and this with increasing efficiency and lower costs.

5.5.2 Structuring of the Solution

For both variants—outsourcing and managed services—it is important to define the service levels in a detailed and consistent manner. The basis for this description has proven itself to map the services relevant IT landscape into a unified structure. With this, service level agreements become comparable; measurable quality and performance criteria can be defined. Moreover, it is good practice to measure key indicators before and after outsourcing, in order to come to an objective basis to assess its success. Particularly in the Anglo-Saxon areas, so-called *value-based pricing* prevails, in which part of the service fee is calculated depending on the achieved value.

In the context of the Horus method, the four-layer model shown in Fig. 5.16 has proven beneficial for structuring an IT landscape. The basis of this model forms the *IT platform* with its hardware, communications, and system software components. The *application software* positions itself atop, consisting of possibly heterogeneous modules which are linked to one another by suitable integration mechanisms. Based on this, *business processes* and *strategies* are identified and re-documented if necessary. A special feature is that the four-layer model also stretches beyond corporate boundaries, allowing virtual entities to be mapped as well.

A managed service systematically aligns itself to this four-layer model so that the aligned services will be accurately offered at each layer. This increases the effectiveness of the services, opening up sustainable cost reductions. Managed services

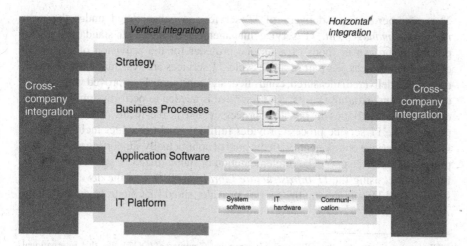

Fig. 5.16 Structuring of an IT landscape: the four-layer model

can be utilized in all phases of the life cycle of an IT environment or solution—also across all levels of the four-layer model. A service client decides himself what support he would like to use in a particular scope, according to his requirements and budget specification. The managed services portfolio extends across all phases of implementing an IT solution, from the initial concept and prototyping to development and commissioning. It contains the operation, including monitoring, administration, and constant solution optimization. A reengineering of the solution follows at the end of the life cycle, as soon as optimization measures achieve only marginal benefit or by strategic considerations. It can involve merely a reengineering of the technical infrastructure or application software but also a genuine business reengineering at business process or strategy level. Here, too, appropriate services are available, including the implementation of simulation studies.

Perhaps the greatest cost reduction potential in the operation of IT solutions, according to experience, slumbers in the introduction of self-service procedures in user support. The interesting thing is that a cost reduction is not only possible through this process but that, in addition, an improved quality of service—for example, by introducing a 24/7 support—can be achieved. For this to be perceived as such by the user, it is important that self-service methods are easily accessible and usable and—at least during a transitional phase—are coupled with traditional support channels. In practice, self-service methods are usually implemented based on Web portals that are placed on an Intranet or the Internet. These Web portals then allocate a variety of service and knowledge management functions, establishing communities of interest through on-line forums and chat rooms. Even interactive training and learning systems can be integrated when needed.

5.5.3   ITIL: Reference Model-Based Service Specification

The customer-oriented delivery of IT services is consolidated under the term *IT service management*. IT service management includes all standardized and practically proven methods of a service provider for the provision of customer-oriented IT services. As part of a life cycle, IT services are systematically planned, developed, delivered, measured, controlled, and continuously improved with respect to internal and external factors. An IT service is needed to perform semiautomated or automated activities in business processes and is the result of an IT service process. The IT service process provides fulfilling qualities under inclusion of IT intelligent service components with the goal of contractually supporting the business process of a service user. The implementation of standardized IT service processes, for example, using the *IT Infrastructure Library* (ITIL[4]), and the development of standardized IT services by the service provider should facilitate faster and more

---

[4]ITIL is maintained by the Office of Government Commerce (OGC), by the International Standardization Organization (ISO), and by the British Standards Institution (BSI). The framework

flexible mapping of the customer requirements in terms of IT support of business processes into the IT service process.

The ITIL framework is a globally established *de facto* standard for IT service management. ITIL suggests what needs to be done for the management of IT services needs, but not how the proposed methods are to be individually implemented. The mode of implementation is left to the respective enterprises themselves. The current ITIL Version 3 consists of the components ITIL Core (guideline for organizations that provide IT services) and ITIL Complementary Guidance (guideline for specific industrial sectors, organization types, operating models, and technical architectures).

The ITIL Core, as the main reference for corporate practice, includes the publications `Service Strategy`, `Service Design`, `Service Transition`, `Service Operation`, and `Continual Service Improvement`. Together, these publications represent the phases of a life cycle for IT services. In addition, strategies for the design and provision of IT services as well as methods for release of IT services in the operational mode are described. Moreover, guidelines for establishing a continuous improvement process are provided. The life cycle of IT services has the objective of continuous learning, improvement, and "maturing" of the organization. The strategy for the provision of IT services lies at the core of the life cycle. Phase `Service Strategy` describes the basic understanding of IT as a strategic asset by providing a guide for how IT service management should be developed and implemented, not only from an organizational design but also from a strategic perspective. As part of the service design phase, a guide for the design and development of IT services and IT service management processes is provided. The implementation of the requirements for new or changed IT services from the `Service Strategy` is addressed in the `Service Transition` phase. The management and operation of IT services take place in the `Service Operation` phase. The continuous improvement process includes the entire life cycle of IT services within the framework of `Continual Service Improvement`. The service provider must implement consistent and repeatable IT service processes to preserve or improve the quality of IT services.

A deficit of ITIL is, however, the informal representation of the proposed IT service processes. A formal model of IT service processes is necessary if qualitative and quantitative analysis is to be conducted. The model types recommended in the Horus method are suitable for precise, graphical modeling of IT service processes. The procedure models in the form of Petri nets form the central point of reference (see Fig. 5.17).

Petri nets are suitable for various reasons, particularly for modeling, analysis, and implementation of IT service processes. Quality characteristics of IT services can also be modeled and simulated by Petri nets, in addition to IT service processes. Moreover, Petri nets allow the modeling of complex process and quality of service

---

has continuously been developed with the assistance of the internationally active "IT Service Management Forum e.V." (itSMF).

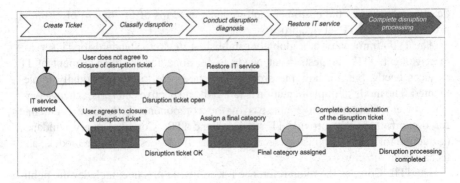

Fig. 5.17 Incident management process modeled with Horus in accordance with ITIL

objects within different process levels, as typically found in IT service processes. Petri nets also support the use of standards for the intra- and intercompany exchange of service-level information and facilitate the standardized development, implementation, and monitoring of relevant key figures. In addition, Petri nets support the representation of systems and IT service processes at various levels of abstraction. IT service processes can be depicted, analyzed, and documented in a user friendly manner with the Horus modeling tool.

5.6   Business Process Outsourcing

Even at the beginning of this millennium traded as a future megatrend in the business world, virtualization strategies have meanwhile developed into common instruments for corporate management. In a business context, virtualization bases on the idea that the enterprise business processes do not necessarily have to be performed by the enterprise itself, but can also be performed by strategic partners. However, the overall process is guided by the virtualized enterprise, which requires close cooperation, and in the subsequent process, presupposes close integration with the strategic partners.

The relocation of business processes as part of a virtualization strategy is referred to as *business process outsourcing* (BPO). By means of BPO, the complete execution of a business process is delegated to a BPO service provider, including all underlying business services. Cost advantages are often strived with BPO, especially if personnel or resource-intensive processes are involved. However, be warned that BPO should not be considered only from a cost perspective. It is more important to look at the BPO decision from the perspective of value creation. Advantages in opening up new markets must be taken into account (e.g., by adding a local distribution partner in the target market) or through the use of specialized knowledge, for example, through special manufacturing processes that introduce strategic manufacturing partners into the value chain. In addition, shorter process cycle times or minimizing process risks are valid considerations in the BPO decision.

5.6.1 Typical Fields of Application

Some important application fields for BPO in practice will be addressed next.

5.6.1.1 Personnel-Intensive Transaction Processing

In many industries, the outsourcing of transaction executing processes involving high personnel intensity has become common practice these days. It offers high savings potential and sustained productivity improvement in the back office, as employees can then focus on more dispositional tasks. The enterprise customers perceive this through competitive prices and improved service quality. Here are some service examples from different industries:

- *Financial services*: Purchasing and accounts payable, order management and accounts receivable, general accounting, travel and expense reports, account reconciliation.
- *Trade*: Logistics, freight invoices, order management, returns, account reconciliation.
- *Insurance*: Quotations, contract conclusion, premium statement, accounts receivable, claims processing.
- *Health care*: Social insurance accounting, processing of reimbursement claims, accounts receivable, rejected reimbursement claims.

5.6.1.2 Knowledge-Intensive Processes

While cost considerations have been paramount in the previously considered examples of BPO, the superior knowledge of a service provider plays an important role in the following examples. In general, the scope of outsourced knowledge-intensive processes and in particular its complexity is significantly higher than the "simple" transaction processing mentioned above. For the end customer, the advantages of BPO knowledge-intensive processes are demonstrated mostly through improved product quality and the accelerated implementation of innovations. A few examples will illustrate this:

- *OEM production*[5]: OEM manufacturers have special—often low cost—resources or special expertise in the manufacturing of "original equipment". Characteristic

---

[5]Original Equipment Manfacturing.

of OEM manufacturers is that they do not bring the produced goods into the market. In many cases, the engineering services or perhaps the necessary tools are provided by the client, or are developed jointly as part of a collaborative engineering process.

- *Contract logistics*: Contractually fixed package of logistics services (transportation, warehousing, refinement, etc.) performed by a logistics service provider for purchasing or sales organizations.
- *Distribution services*: The service provider takes over the distribution of certain products in a clearly defined target market. Often, distribution is not limited to the marketing of the products but includes marketing, warehousing, and often end-customer service.
- *Contact center*: Qualified service providers operate entire contact centers on behalf of the customers. Multimodal and multilingual inbound and outbound services are offered. Typical inbound services include customer service and care (loyalty, commitment, satisfaction) or internal IT help desks for technical and user support. Typical outbound services include campaign management and telemarketing, telesales, sales support (appointments), telemarket research, or also multimodal dunning processes. Up and cross-selling opportunities are put to full use with a high level of expertise.
- *Personnel management and earnings*: A very common application for BPO is personnel management (full recruit-to-retire processes) and especially the settlement of wage and salary statements. Although cost considerations indeed play a role in the personnel area, the high level of expertise and the service provider's ability to remain in a current state of knowledge stands in the foreground of BPO.

5.6.1.3   Exploitation of Location Advantages

Location advantages of a service provider are utilized in many applications of knowledge-intensive processes. For example, an outsourced assembly at the customer location can lead directly to cost advantages, shorter delivery times, intensified customer loyalty, and hence to competitive advantages. The situation is similar if contract logistics, with the operation of a warehouse near the customer or the supplier, is included. Alternatively, the distribution services are delivered into a local target market in which the commissioned sales organization itself is not represented.

5.6.2   *Basic Principle of Business Process Outsourcing*

BPO follows a basic principle which is shown in Fig. 5.17. A sample scenario is illustrated in which three BPO service customers outsource a process to the BPO service provider. Due to specific business requirements on the customer's side, the problem for the service provider arises that the outsourced processes are not identical. This has very significant challenges for his flexibility, without which he will not be competitive in the market. In addition, he has to act very cost-sensitively, focusing his capabilities on the best customer value. A suitable solution is the Horus Business Process Management architecture presented in Sect. 4.5, which separates the implementation-oriented business services from the customer-specific business processes. Incidentally, the implementation of customer business processes on a homogeneous service layer presents, in itself, a form of virtualization.

Process costs typically are at the center of economic BPO studies. They are compared with the expected benefits in order to come to a resilient basis for decision. One must not forget that BPO always raises technical issues. How does the integration of the outsourced business processes with internal processes or other outsourced processes take place? How are corporation-wide processes realized beyond corporate boundaries, and how does the overall process control take place? Can business activity monitoring be guaranteed across all processes? Who will ensure compliance of business rules within the overall context of the virtual enterprise? How will a uniform and consistent master data management be ensured? Are collaborative planning processes, involving all participating business partners, including customers and suppliers provided for? The sheer quantity of these issues shows that in the initial technical implementation of the BPO, and in the current operation, significant cost drivers can be found.

Integration components in the form of a *mediation layer* are shown in Fig. 5.18. A mediation layer is spoken of since the service provider strives rising economies

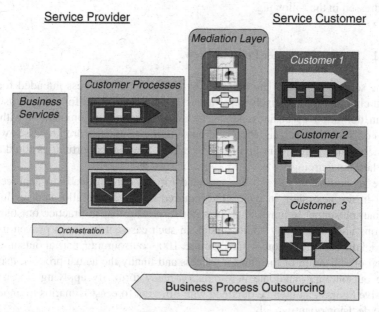

Fig. 5.18 Basic principle of business process outsourcing (BPO)

of scale and will therefore always try to handle all of the outsourced processes as consistently as possible internally. This is reflected in largely standardized procedures with appropriate control and data flows. On the other hand, since the service customer expects his individual requirements to be implemented, a customer-specific transformation of the control and data flow exchanged between service providers and service customer must take place in the mediation layer. BPO service customers also demand—not least of all due to GRC requirements (see Sect. 5.4)—a degree of transparency regarding not only the process results but also the process execution itself. Accordingly, the service provider is required to offer customized reporting, meaningful key indicators, and analysis.

5.6.3   Model-Based Planning and Implementation of BPO Contracts

As the name suggests, BPO is all about business processes, so that BPO is a "natural" field of application for the Horus method and the Horus tools. And this applies across the entire life cycle of BPO contracts. In addition, it should more than be clear from the foregoing statements that BPO requires a common understanding of the technical business requirements between service customer and service provider, generated by the outsourced process to be implemented. This common understanding can be specified in a formal way by means of Horus models. How Horus can be used by parties involved with BPO and the resulting benefits will be addressed in the following.

5.6.3.1   Service Customer Point of View

For the service customer, the first task is to identify the process intended for the outsourcing and to selectively separate it. The starting points for this are usually a clean definition of business strategies and objectives in conjunction with the results of a SWOT analysis. Preferred outsourcing candidates are processes where weaknesses have been identified in their context or where opportunities could arise from their outsourcing.

The separation of the process intended for outsourcing leads to a procedure model in the next step, in which the required resources are allocated, including the exact personnel requirements. It is not surprising that in practice outsourcing decisions are often highly controversial. In such cases, it has been proven useful to model different variations—for example, 100% outsourcing, partial outsourcing, internal optimization of the current process and finally the actual process, itself—of the outsourcing candidate in simulation-ready form. By applying simulation, extensive figures can then be obtained with different forecast scenarios to underlay a BPO decision quantitatively.

From the simulation and internal feasibility studies, a model-based specification of the business process to be outsourced will result. This specification should include the expected features of the process—costs, time, added value, quality—also the relevant business objects and a key indicator system by which the performance of the process is measured. The process specification then forms the core of a specification book based on which a provider selection and call for bid takes place for the BPO.

5.6.3.2 Service Provider Point of View

For the service provider, working with Horus models offers starting points in the market-oriented design of the "process offer," subsequently in the sales process and the implementation of the acquired outsourcing contracts.

First, it is recommended that the service provider separates the reusable business services provided to him from the industry and customer-specific business processes, as presented in Sect. 4.5 where the Horus BPM architecture has been proposed. This has the advantage that in customer-specific adaptations of the offered business process, the businesses services can further be used, mostly unchanged. Based on this, the service provider creates several industry-specific process templates to support their marketing and sales. These templates are ideal to show potential customers the performance and benefits of BPO. As experience shows, different forecasts of the process load to be expected are based on such benefit analysis. It is obvious that simulation can be a valuable service in such benefit analysis. In addition, an animation of simulation runs as part of sales presentations has proven to be a convincing visualization tool.

Horus models also come to use as part of the proposal and, above all, the specification preparation. They are used for the formal specification of the services scope and contain, in addition to the procedure models, resource, business object, and key indicator definitions. By the way, a so-called *value-based pricing* can be achieved based on these statements, that is, pricing based on the actual benefit that is generated by BPO.

5.6.3.3 The Importance of Industry Reference Models

The considerations for the use of models throughout the entire BPO contract cycle—from the suitable offer on the market over the tendering and bid management to implementation of the agreement—reveal a significant weakness. It arises from the need to compare models that are created on the supplier and customer side, even bringing them into congruence if necessary. This can be an arbitrarily complex, and in any case, time consuming process. General reference models may solve this, as offered by industry associations, for example. In Sect. 5.1.4, the enhanced Telecom Operations Map® (short: eTOM®) of the TeleManagement Forum and the SCOR® Supply Chain Operations Reference Model of the Supply Chain Council were mentioned as appropriate examples. These reference models can then be used by both parties as a common reference point. It is thus obvious that the mutual adjustment of the models is much easier with this.

5.7 Self-Control

Exercise 5.1. Consider Fig. 5.3 with regard to a commercial enterprise that operates both a stationary as well as an electronic business. Formulate objectives and strategies for this enterprise for goal achievement. Then try to operationalize this via key figures.

Exercise 5.2. Model-based business process reengineering has several similarities with the construction of a house: After many years in your current home, you decide to build a new one, providing the specifications to your contractor in several ways:

• The desired properties of the new house can be specified using the old one.
• You take in the requirements, put them in a plan or even in a prototype (a model), and design the new house based on this.

Explain why each of these approaches probably will result in a different house.

Exercise 5.3. Consider Fig. 5.6 and name various enterprise-wide business processes from the B2B and the B2C sector for the commercial enterprise considered in Fig. 5.1. In the future, the enterprise would like to offer special discounts to authorities; a connection to authorities via an ESB shall take place for this. How can the enterprise collaborate with one or more development partners?

Exercise 5.4. Explain the role of a key user in the introduction of business software. Also, consider how he will proceed when using Horus; compare this with a procedure for the exclusive use of common office tools. What risks arise from this?

Exercise 5.5. Governance, risk, and compliance are often mentioned together. Explain the relationships between these concepts in an IT context, describing from what a significant importance arises for top management.

Exercise 5.6. Consider what advantages and disadvantages arise for an enterprise through an alignment of its IT services with the ITIL standard.

Exercise 5.7. Name examples for business process outsourcing. In each case, indicate what potential benefits you are able to recognize (costs, faster processes, better product quality, etc.).

5.8 Bibliographic References and Web Links

References were already given in previous chapters for business process reengineering, for example, Hammer and Champy (1993). Becker and Delfmann (2007) cover the area of reference modeling as well as procedure models for domain-related customizing. Procedure models are widely used in information technology, for example, in quality management, in project management, and particularly in software development; see, for example, Chemuturi and Cagley (2010). For SOAs, consult Erl (2005, 2009) or Singh and Huhns (2005).

The topics of IT Governance and ITIL are evidently closely related and are therefore often covered together; compare, for example, Van Grembergen and Dehaes (2007). The *IT Infrastructure Library* (ITIL) was developed in the late eighties in the context that organizations are increasingly becoming dependent on IT, and that business objectives can be achieved only through an efficient use of IT. A management concept was to be created on behalf of the British government, unifying and documenting IT service processes in order to improve the management and control of IT in public administration. The management concept to be developed should also demonstrate appropriate and efficient methods to improve IT services sustainably, while reducing their operating costs. Although originally created for public administrations, it soon became clear that the management concept could be transferred to IT organizations from other industries based on its abstractness. Numerous Books have been published about ITIL; for starters, see Persse (2010). Section 5.5.3 originates from Dr. Christian Bartsch. Further information on ITIL can be found in his (German) dissertation, Bartsch (2010). On the subject of virtualization, compare Menken (2010).

The text of this chapter mentions the following entities and organizations, where further information can be found on the Web:

- TeleManagement Forum: www.tmforum.com
- TM Forum Business Process Framework (eTOM):
  www.tmforum.org/BusinessProcessFramework/1647/home.html
- Supply Chain Council: www.supply-chain.org
- Supply Chain Operations Reference model (SCOR®):
  supply-chain.org/about/scor/what/is
- Web Services Description Language (WSDL): www.w3.org/TR/wsdl
- Office of Government Commerce (OGC): www.ogc.gov.uk
- International Organization for Standardization (ISO): www.iso.org
- British Standards Institution (BSI): www.bsigroup.com
- IT Service Management Forum Deutschland e.V. (itSMF): www.itsmf.de

Chapter 6
On the Future of Business Process Engineering

In this concluding chapter, we gather several thoughts on how the future of business process engineering might look like. Topics and technologies that from our perspective will definitely have an impact include virtual worlds and 3D graphics on the one hand, and socialization on the other. The latter has been brought along by Web 2.0 developments and is now vastly exploited in many areas of information technology. Last, not least, adding semantic information will play a significant role in future BPM.

6.1 Virtual Worlds

The benefit of a business process model essentially depends on the extent to which business users can correctly interpret it. This initially requires a certain degree of structuring assets that will enable a user to understand model elements and their use for the structuring of related models. Experience shows that this will cause few problems in connection with simple graphical models. For users, however, it is difficult to transfer the models to their real business world. Users often feel overwhelmed in light of the presupposed abilities for the abstraction. The result is that business process models are rejected, or at least that their benefits are significantly affected within the framework of project communication or in user training. Based on the advanced visualization capabilities of modern games, an approach is therefore pursued to enable the run-through of processes in virtual worlds. In a virtual world, a real-world extract (e.g., a production line, an office space) is realistically simulated and graphically visualized. Various task carriers can be integrated as avatars in the virtual world. Process model simulation in this context means to execute the procedure of a business process including the required interaction with the avatars. Due to the realistic visualization of a business process and its environment, it is possible even for untrained personnel to understand the process flow or to examine a given process model with regard to correct mapping.

F. Schönthaler et al., *Business Processes for Business Communities*,
DOI 10.1007/978-3-642-24791-0_6, © Springer-Verlag Berlin Heidelberg 2012

The control of the procedure and avatars can take place with a joystick, or a novel input device, such as a data glove or a touch panel. For example, the visualization of the virtual world can take place with 3D glasses that allow a spatial representation. The basis for process simulation in a virtual world is a sufficiently accurate process model with information about the process flow, a model of the required avatars, and an adequate model of the process environment.

6.2   Three-Dimensional Process Models

The graphical representation of a process on a screen or on paper becomes confusing beyond a certain degree of complexity or a high degree of detail. By focusing on individual aspects of interest (views) such as roles, resources, or activities, the complexity of the representation (i.e., the amount of information displayed) is reduced. Coherences between the representations are lost, particularly during depiction.

New approaches in graphical representation of process models therefore include, in a given base model of the procedure, additional information portrayed as extra dimensions in the graphic representation of a process. This form of representation is particularly suitable for the representation of roles, time, and resources in the process model. The 3D portrayal can be simulated in an imaginary space on a screen through mapping that is spanned by three axes.

It is also possible, however, in order to improve the spatial representation; instead of an image on a flat surface, visualize the imaginary space of the process model with 3D glasses. In particular, simulation runs can therefore be visualized in the form of a "flight" over or through the 3D process model.

6.3   Semantic Processes

Semantic business process management is based on the idea of enriching business process models with additional metainformation ("knowledge") to support a mechanized, that is, automated processing of the models. Additional information can affect all components of process models, such as activities, resources, or roles, or the process as a whole. The additional information is usually provided in the form of *ontologies*. Simply put, ontologies represent terms of an application context in the sense of a formal presentation, together with relationships between the terms. Ontologies enable, for example, the explicit use of terms that otherwise would be ambiguous and therefore not be accurately interpretable (due to the problematic nature of synonyms). With the information contained in the ontology regarding relationships between concepts, automated analysis and conclusions can be made.

For semantic business process management, there are three important application scenarios:

1. Finding appropriate process models in a process model library: A typical query might be: Find all the process models in which orders are processed. If it is documented in the ontology that `Purchase order` and `Order` are synonyms, the request would automatically find process models that process the orders. The user making the request need not to know these relationships.
2. Supporting the modeler in the editing process, as defined by autocompletion, where suggestions are made as to how a given process model fragment can be supplemented: If a process model fragment generates a particular object as output, for example, then such process fragments can be proposed to the modeler, in which this object is input. Information about the application context can also be taken into account, in which existing process model fragments have thus far been applied. In addition, specific recommendations or specific quality statements from other modelers can be used during editing.
3. Coupling of process models from different enterprises (or different areas of an enterprise) to one other: Typically, enterprises use different terminologies when describing their business processes and business objects. A special case is when enterprises use words from different languages (such as German and English). Business objects are exchanged at the interface between the two enterprises. Ontologies can be used to uniquely identify these objects (and the generating or processing activities). Typically, such ontologies are industry specific, that is, different ontologies exist for different industries. If different enterprises use different modeling languages to describe their business processes, ontologies can then also be used in the automatic translation of models from one language to the other or with the coupling of different models.

Semantic business process management requires specific enhancements to modeling languages, methods, and tools.

6.4 Social BPM

Modeling languages, methods, and tools have been described in this book that are suitable to design business processes thoroughly and with a high degree of quality. The term *business process engineering* which we use in this context expresses the fact that this is first and foremost an *engineering* approach. Moreover, an engineering approach implies that the instruments used are controlled and can be used effectively and, ideally, efficiently as well. We also use the term "design" to make it clear that creative elements come into play: New paths have to be taken that are reflected in genuine process innovations. The preoccupation with business processes often leads to completely new services, serves as a catalyst for new products, or sets the foundation for new business models.

The benefits of a business process model is greatest when the knowledge and creativity reflects all people involved, whether they are internal employees of an enterprise, employees of partner enterprises, or generally people whose knowledge can contribute to the design of the business process, either directly or indirectly.

Either way, it is clear in this context that not only expertise but also sometimes "merely" the much-cited ounce of common sense is in demand. In short, the goal of business process engineering is not only to create business processes for a business community but also to use the knowledge of an entire business community—and beyond—in the shaping of the processes. But how can this goal of participation be achieved? How can we succeed in getting people with very different structuring and abstraction abilities involved in business process engineering (BPE)? Moreover, how do we encounter the dangers that arise from the fact that people follow different objectives during their participation, which in many cases are not even compatible with each other? *Social* BPE, or more generally put *social* BPM (business process management), will attempt to provide an answer to these questions.

6.4.1   Socialization of Business Process Management

Social BPM is based on the idea that business process management is not the task of an individual or a selected group—think here of the coordination department or selflessly fighting staff departments—but is a responsibility of the entire business community, which consists of the entire enterprise, and possibly all involved business partners and external knowledge carriers. BPM itself thus becomes a collaborative process, and its quality depends largely upon the quality of collaboration, in terms of work efficiency and quality of results. In addition to the sociological components, the communication possibilities within the business community play a key role here.

If you take a look into the behavior of today's youth, the solution is obvious: social networks with the technical capabilities of Web 2.0. For young people, collaboration in Web-based social networks is a matter of course. Moreover, the willingness to contribute within the community for the solution of problems, often under a very high time expenditure, is extremely large. In spite of all risks (often discussed elsewhere) that may arise from the ever-spreading social networks, the commitment and creative power that is applied by collaborative community members is very impressive. And this form of collaboration is the foundation of social BPM.

The starting point for social BPM is the socialization of business process design: social business process engineering (social BPE). The members of the business communities involved have access to modeling, simulation, analysis, and evaluation of business processes using software tools. In Web 2.0-based social networks, they exchange models, discussing and checking them. In many cases, there are also "special interest groups" whose members model and simulate on the Web together. The advantage is obvious: The participation of all community members in conjunction with powerful business process software ensures a high quality of the resulting business process models.

Social BPM does not end with the design process, but goes much further, right into the execution of processes. The aim of socializing the process execution—we are talking about *social business process execution* (social BPX) here—is an optimal usability of application services for business communities, from user groups right down to individual users. This is achieved by providing context-sensitive Web 2.0 portals, which offer user appropriate features for the personalization of the portals. Many manufacturers in the IT industry often use the term Enterprise 2.0 in this context, indicating the use of Web 2.0 technologies and concepts in the corporate context.

In the following, we will not elaborate further on aspects of social BPX, as this is beyond the scope of this book. In our considerations, we also must put greater emphasis on the potentials that lie in the socialization of the design and use of business process models.

6.4.2 Web 2.0 Infrastructure for Social BPM

Social BPM requires a technical infrastructure in which the common interaction possibilities of Web 2.0 can be used. Different devices should be integrated here, in particular mobile devices right up to smart phones and pads in business sectors. Infrastructures are established in these communities, where the collaborative design or sharing of business processes takes place. Private communities are distinguished on the basis of Intranets and public communities, which are available on the Internet. Figure 6.1 outlines a typical Social BPM infrastructure.

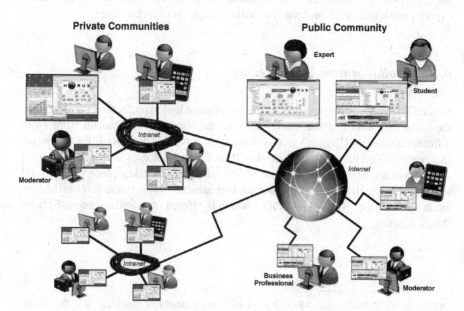

Fig. 6.1 Typical social BPM infrastructure

In a private community, members work together in a "closed" business community. The private community includes employees in an organizational unit, an entire organization, a consortium, a virtual enterprise, and sometimes business partner employees. Permanent and temporary community members can be distinguished in a private community. Temporary members will receive access to the community only for a certain period of time or for a specific task. It is clear that a social BPM infrastructure—particularly in the context of business communities—presupposes a sophisticated access management system with identity management. A further prerequisite is one or more moderators, as compliance with the stipulated rules within the community cannot be enforced only with technical capabilities. In addition, the moderators should ensure that the business community actually achieves the objectives set within the context of collaborative work.

This is where private and public communities differ. Moderators in *public communities* usually have no right to drive the collaboration into a particular direction. This law behooves exclusively the community itself—under a given code of conduct within the community. For *public communities*, it is typical that business professionals, protagonists from research and education, as well as students are to be found. Interdisciplinary work is typical. Moreover, exactly this characteristic environment signifies the public community for business process innovation and creative ideas for solutions.

By the way, a new kind of service, which we will call "BPM Consulting on Demand," is developing in BPM. This particular form of consulting is provided by experts working on the requirements within the community. Costs are involved with the expert's services, so it must be regulated within the community, which costs the expert's work will incur, and who is entitled to call on expert services.

6.4.3   Collaborative Transactions

Social BPM has been recognized by major software tool manufacturers as a topic of the future. As a look at the market shows, manufacturers view social BPM from different angles. ARISalign[1] is positioned "as a type of Facebook for business" (Software AG). The platform combines Web 2.0 technologies with modeling tool ARIS Express. The collaborative modeling of processes takes place on a virtual white board, which can then be exported. Infrastructure aspects and fast availability are at the forefront with SIGNAVIO,[2] which is offered on a Software-as-a-Service (SaaS) basis.

---

[1] ARISalign™, ARIS®, and ARIS® Express™ are products of Software AG, Darmstadt, Germany.
[2] SIGNAVIO® is a product of Signavio GmbH, Berlin, Germany.

Horus[3] describes a more comprehensive approach to social BPM that goes beyond the designation of a collaboration platform, where Web 2.0 functionalities are combined with modeling and simulation tools. Rather, standard tools are equipped with functionalities ("Web 2.0 enabled") that enable users to perform full collaborative transactions. In practice, the situation is such that the user is free to decide, in every phase of his work, whether he utilizes the community's help or if he provides services to the community.

The most important relevant collaborative transactions, in the context of social BPM, can be classified as follows:

- *Community.* Development of a Web 2.0 community by tagging, linking, news and feeds, presence and instant messaging, chat, discussion forums, blogging, and microblogging (Twitter). Establishment of subcommunities (Special Interest Groups).
- *Workflows and task management.* Definition and management of tasks in the creation and use of models. In addition, predefined workflows form multilevel review and approval processes.
- *Distributed modeling.* Dismantling of modeling tasks into subtasks that are then carried out by different people. Workflows and integration capabilities ensure that modeling results can be merged later.
- *Collaborative working.* Collaborative modeling, presentation, and simulation of business process models.
- *Knowledge management.* Integration of business process models and wikis. Commenting, evaluating, and rating of models. Identification of knowledge sources. Flexible search capabilities on all model details and in the entire business community content.
- *Model and knowledge exchange.* Models can be offered and traded as best practice solutions. In addition, experts can offer their expertise to the community. The Exchange features can be interpreted as either free or paid services.

With the advancement of Web technologies, new opportunities constantly arise in applications within social BPM. The practical application will show which functions provide the highest benefit for the business community.

6.5 Self-Control

Exercise 6.1. Explain the abstract collaborative transactions presented in this chapter using specific examples.

Exercise 6.2. Consider which sociological problems might arise from Social BPM or Social BPE, especially if they are used in a business context.

---

[3]Horus® is a product of Horus software GmbH, Ettlingen, Germany.

6.6   Bibliographic Notes

Virtual worlds and 3D models are discussed by Eichhorn et al. (2009). Vossen and Hagemann (2007) give a basic introduction to various aspects of Web 2.0; see also Vossen (2009) as well as Dawson (2009). Semantic processes are addressed, inter alia, by Betz et al. (2006) as well as Koschmider and Oberweis (2010).

Bibliography

Bartsch C (2010) Modellierung und simulation von IT-dienstleistungsprozessen. KIT Scientific, Karlsruhe

Becker J, Delfmann P (2007) Reference modeling: efficient information systems design through reuse of information models. Physica-Verlag, Heidelberg

Becker J, Kugeler M, Rosemann M (2011) Process management: a guide for the design of business processes, 2nd edn. Springer, Berlin

Betz S, Klink S, Koschmider A, Oberweis A (2006) Automatic user support for business process modeling. In: Hinkelmann K, Karagiannis D, Stojanovic N, Wagner G (eds) Proceedings of the workshop on semantics for business process management at the 3rd European semantic web conference, Budva/Montenegro, pp 1–12

vom Brocke J, Rosemann M (eds) (2010) Handbook on business process management, vols 1 and 2. Spinger, Berlin

Chemuturi MK, Cagley TM (2010) Mastering software project management: best practices, tools and techniques. J. Ross, Fort Lauderdale

Chen PP-S (1976) The entity-relationship model – toward a unified view of data. ACM Trans Database Syst 1:9–36

Daum B (2003) Modeling business objects with XML schema. Morgan Kaufmann, Burlington

Davis R (2001) Business process modelling with ARIS: a practical guide. Springer, Berlin

Davis R (2008) ARIS design platform: advanced process modelling and administration. Springer, Berlin

Davis R, Brabander E (2007) ARIS design platform: getting started with BPM. Springer, Berlin

Dawson R (2009) Implementing enterprise 2.0: a practical guide to creating business value inside organizations with web technologies. CreateSpace On-Demand Publishing. www.createspace.com

Dutton JE (1993) Commonsense approach to process modeling. IEEE Software 10(4):56–64

Eichhorn D, Koschmider A, Li Y, Oberweis A, Stürzel P, Trunko R (2009) 3D Support for business process simulation. In: Ahamed SI et al. (eds) Proceedings of the 33rd annual IEEE international computer software and applications conference (COMPSAC 2009), IEEE Computer Society, Seattle, pp 73–80

Erl T (2005) Service-oriented architecture (SOA): concepts, technology, and design. Prentice-Hall, Upper Saddle River

Erl T (2009) SOA desing patterns. Prentice-Hall, Upper Saddle River

Fine LG (2009) The SWOT analysis: using your strength to overcome weaknesses, using opportunities to overcome threats. CreateSpace On-Demand Publishing. www.createspace.com

Garcia-Molina H, Ullman JD, Widom J (2008) Database systems: the complete book, 2nd edn. Prentice-Hall, Upper Saddle River

Grosskopf A, Decker G, Weske M (2009) The process: business process modeling using BPMN. Meghan-Kiffer, Tampa. www.mkpress.com

Hammer M, Champy JA (1993) Reengineering the corporation: a manifesto for business revolution. (überarbeitete Ausgabe Dezember 2003) Harper Collins, New York

Harvey M (2005) Essential business process modeling. O'Reilly Media, Sebastopol

Kaplan RS, Norton DP (1992) The balanced scorecard: measures that drive performance. Harv Bus Rev:71–80

Kaplan RS, Norton DP (1993) Putting the balanced scorecard to work. Harv Bus Rev:2–16

Kaplan RS, Norton DP (1996) The balanced scorecard: translating strategy into action. Harvard Business School Publishing, Boston

Kaplan RS, Norton DP (2000) The strategy-focused organization. Harvard Business School Publishing Corp., Boston

Kaplan RS, Norton DP (2008) The execution premium: linking strategy to operations for competitive advantage. Harvard Business School Publishing, Boston

Koschmider A, Oberweis A (2010) Designing business processes with a recommendation-based editor. In: Rosemann M, vom Brocke J (eds) Handbook on business process management, vol 1. Springer, Berlin

Lenz K (2002) Modeling a execution of E-business processes using XML nets. Dissertation, Goethe-Universität Frankfurt, Fachbereich Wirtschaftswissenschaften (in German)

Lenz K, Oberweis A (2003) Inter-organizational business process management with XML nets. In: Ehrig H, Reisig W, Rozenberg G, Weber H (eds) Petri net technology for communication-based systems – advances in Petri nets. LNCS 2472. Spinger, Berlin, pp 243–263

Menken I (2010) Virtualization – the complete cornerstone guide to virtualization best practices, 2nd edn. Emereo, Newstead

Persse JR (2010) A basic approach to ITIL service operation: setting the foundation for ITIL V3. Tree of Press, Atlanta

Petri CA (1962) Communication with automata. Schriften des Rheinisch-Westfälischen Instituts für Instrumentelle Mathematik an der Universität Bonn, Heft 2 (in German)

Podeswa H (2009) UML for the IT business analyst, 2nd edn. Course Technology PTR, Boston

Reisig W (2011) Petri nets. In: Koch I, Reisig W, Schreiber F (eds) Modeling in systems biology, the Petri net approach. Springer, Berlin

Rosenberg D, Stephens M (2007) Use case driven object modeling with UML: theory and practice. Apress, New York

Ross SM (2006) Simulation, 4th edn. Academic, San Diego

Scheer A-W (2000a) ARIS: business process modeling, 3rd edn. Springer, Berlin

Scheer A-W (2000b) ARIS: business process frameworks, 3rd edn. Springer, Berlin

Scheer A-W, Abolhassan F, Jost W, Kirchmer M (2002) Hrsg, Business process excellence – ARIS in practice. Spinger, Berlin

Silberschatz A, Korth HF, Sudarshan S (2010) Database system concepts, 6th edn. McGraw-Hill, New York

Singh MP, Huhns MN (2005) Service-oriented computing – semantics, processes, agents. Wiley, New York

Sokolowski JA, Banks CM (2009) Principles of modeling and simulation: a multidisciplinary approach. Wiley, New York

Van der Aalst W, Ter Hofstede A, Kiepuszewski B, Barros AP (2003) Workflow patterns. Distrib Parallel Database 14(1):5–51

Van der Aalst W, Van Hee K (2004) Workflow management: models, methods, and systems. MIT, Boston

Van Grembergen W, Dehaes S (2007) Implementing information technology governance: models, practices and cases. IGI, Hershey

Vonhoegen H (2009) Einstieg in XML: aktuelle standards: XML schema, XSL, XLink. Galileo Press, Bonn

Vose D (2008) Risk analysis: a quantitative guide. Wiley, New York

Vossen G (2009) Web 2.0: a Buzzword, a serious development, just fun, or what? Proceeings of the international conference on e-Business (ICE-B), Milan, pp IS-33–IS-40

Vossen G, Hagemann S (2007) Unleashing Web 2.0 – from concepts to creativity. Morgan Kaufmann, Burlington

Weitz W (1999) Integrated document and process modeling in electronic commerce. Dissertation, University of Karlsruhe (TH), Fakultät für Wirtschaftswissenschaften (in German)

Weske M (2007) Business process management: concepts, languages, architectures. Springer, Berlin

Index